metal style

20 jewelry designs with cold join techniques

Karen Dougherty

INTERWEAVE.
interweave.com

For Robert J. Dougherty III, my beautiful brother.

I will always love you, my angel Robert. You're with me every moment. I won't ever stop missing you. Your sweet smile, your twinkly eyes, your giggle, your hugs, your voice. The kindest brother, the sweetest son, the proudest father. The most lovely man. We were so lucky to be loved by you. My sorrow for you is immeasurable.

You are forever in my heart.

TECHNICAL EDITOR: Jane Dickerson
ART DIRECTOR: Liz Quan
DESIGNER: Julia Boyles
PHOTO STYLIST: Allie Liebgott
PHOTOGRAPHY: Brad Bartholomew, except
   pages 9–15 and 17–25 by Jim Lawson
STEP PHOTOGRAPHY: Contributing artists
PRODUCTION: Katherine Jackson

Interweave Press LLC
201 East Fourth Street
Loveland, CO 80537-5655
interweave.com

Printed in China by Asia Pacific Offset Ltd.

Library of Congress Cataloging-in-Publication Data

Dougherty, Karen.
Metal style : 20 jewelry designs with cold join techniques :
learn to create stunning metal jewelry using simple cold-join
techniques from top jewelry designers / Karen Dougherty.
   p. cm.
Includes index.
ISBN 978-1-59668-282-5 [pbk.]
ISBN 978-1-59668-494-2 [eBook]
1. Jewelry making. 2. Metal-work. I. Title.
TT212.D68 2011
739.27--dc22
2010030728

10 9 8 7 6 5 4 3 2

Acknowledgments

For my mother and father, who have opened all the doors for me—I am forever grateful for your support, encouragement, and love.

Thank you to my daughters, Gina and Reese, for your patience and to my husband for the hours you gave. For all my friends, thank you for your encouragement and support. I am a lucky girl to love you all. You know who you are.

Contents

Projects

The term "cold connections" means to join
or "cold join" materials without the use
of flame or solder. No heat means more
design possibilities! Using a cold join,
you are able to join materials that might
otherwise melt in the soldering process.

No Torch Required!

I started making cold-connected jewelry with a cordless drill, some scrap metal, copper wire, tubing, and drill bits from the hardware store. If you look around, you'll notice cold joins in everyday objects. From door hinges to staples, a variety of simple mechanics abound for you to adapt to your jewelry designs.

You'll learn there are times when joins function and times when they are used purely for decoration. You probably already have a lot of the tools and maybe some materials you need to make the jewelry you'll see in *Metal Style*. You can accomplish a lot of the techniques with common household tools and local hardware store finds. Of course, there are some great tools you'll want to add to your assortment, but they're not necessary to get started.

On the following pages, you'll find ways to transfer your designs to your materials, read about tools that the artists use to create their jewelry, and explore interesting techniques to get the work done. I hope you are inspired by the range of creativity from this talented group of artists.

Tools

My husband likes to say, if you're having a hard time getting work done, it's because you're using the wrong tool. Words to live by. I've been collecting tools for years now, and I still keep a little list of the ones I'd like to add to my arsenal. I try to use what I have and just be happy with my collection, but let's face it, if you're making jewelry, you'll always want at least one more tool.

You'll find an ideal collection of jewelry studio tools on the following pages. However, you don't need all of them. Feel free to improvise, have fun, and be creative with what you have.

Safety

Safety first. In order to make the fabulous jewelry you see here in *Metal Style,* you'll be drilling a lot of holes in sheet metal and perhaps some other materials. Protect your eyes from flying bits when you drill by wearing SAFETY GLASSES. Protect your lungs with a MASK when you're filing or sanding. Little metal bits in your lungs will never make their way out once they're in. Be kind to your ears, and wear EARPLUGS when you are banging and pounding your metal [figure 1].

Work Surface

Set up a work surface that you're comfortable with. Ideally you'll need a DRILLING SURFACE [figure 2]. Clamp a piece of scrap wood to your work surface with a C-CLAMP [figure 3] and save your BENCH PIN [figure 4]. You'll also need a METAL ANVIL [figure 5] or STEEL BENCH BLOCK [figure 2] for punching and texturing. I asked a local welder for a piece of stainless steel, and he gave me a piece at no charge. I also just got an old piece of railroad track from a friend that I'm excited to clean up and try out.

A BENCH PIN [figure 4] is an ideal work surface to brace your work on or against when you need to file or saw interior and exterior shapes in sheet metal. A VISE [figure 6] will also come in handy. I have a clamp-on type that is portable and swivels.

RING CLAMPS [figure 7] are an affordable and essential bench tool for cold connections. The mouth of the clamp is leather lined, and the grip amazes me. Simply slip your metal piece in the jaws of either end, and insert the wedge of wood in the other. Give it a hearty tap on the wedge end, on a metal surface, and your clamped piece will not budge. You can also brace the loaded ring clamp up against your bench pin to steady your work when you need to file.

A CURVED BURNISHER [figure 8] is a great tool for shining up surfaces, and PRONG PUSHERS [figure 9] and BEZEL ROLLERS [figure 10] are great for all kinds of smooth surface shaping (and punching) aside from what they're really made for.

Texturing Tools

The hammers shown are an ideal set for any jewelry maker. A RAWHIDE MALLET [figure 1] provides a wide cushioned blow and won't make surface marks on your sheet like metal hammers do. They're great for forming sheet metal around a bracelet mandrel or a ring band around a ring mandrel. A CHASING HAMMER [figure 2] has a rounded "peen" head some artists use for riveting and texturing. The flatter, smooth head is meant for chasing sheet metal. PLANISHING HAMMERS [figure 3] have a slightly rounded head and are made to smooth and harden sheet. They make a nice subtle texture, too.

You can use a GOLDSMITH'S HAMMER [figure 4] for shaping and riveting, too. It will hammer a rivet flat so it blends right in with the surface of the metal. The flat side of a BALL-PEEN HAMMER [figure 5] is ideal for flattening, as is a nylon-headed hammer. The NYLON-HEADED HAMMER [figure 6] will not leave any surface marks. A RIVETING HAMMER [figure 7] feels delicate and is all you need to form great rivets. My favorite TEXTURING HAMMER [figure 8] these days is shown here. It has a circle pattern on one head and stripes on the other. I use it so much that the head is coming loose. I have some nice FRETZ HAMMERS [figure 9] that make really pretty marks.

MANDRELS [figure 10] are handy forming tools. When used with a rawhide mallet, they provide a perfect surface for forming bracelet, ring and bezel shapes, and jump rings.

CHASING PUNCHES [figure 11] are traditionally used to form or "chase" metal into shapes, a more advanced jewelry technique than what is shown in this book. However, some of the contributing artists use their chasing tools to decorate the surfaces of their metals.

Texturing the surface of your metal can be achieved in so many ways. DECORATIVE PUNCHES [figure 12] are an easy way to achieve really nice markings. If you have an alphabet stamp set, make a mark or put a piece of tape on the thumb side, so you always hold them in the right direction. You can also make your own shapes with steel wire and bang them into sheet metal. Basically, if you're willing to hit it with a hammer, you can probably mark soft metal with it.

Another great tool for texturing sheet metal is an INDUSTRIAL TUBE WRINGER [figure 13].

10

11

12

13

Pliers

A great hand tool set will include assorted pliers used for gripping, bending, cutting, and shaping wire and sheet metal. FLUSH CUTTERS [figure 1] are necessary for nipping riveting wire. TAPERED ROUND-NOSE PLIERS [figure 2] are perfect for making jump rings and rounded loops in your finished jewelry. CHAIN-NOSE PLIERS [figure 3] have a flattened interior and are good for making

an angled bend in wire as well as for general gripping. I use them to open and close jump rings. FLAT-NOSE PLIERS [figure 4] are great for gripping, straightening, and angled bending. These pliers all let you get into small spaces and are desirable on any jewelry-making bench. The WRAP AND TAP TOOL [figure 5] is useful for forming wire and sheet metal into rings and ring shanks.

PARALLEL-ACTION PLIERS' [figures 6a–c] jaws remain parallel as you open and close them. They let you put pressure on an object and hold it at the same time. FORMING PLIERS [figures 6d–e] come in all sorts of interesting tip shapes and are used for making curved wire shapes and ring shanks.

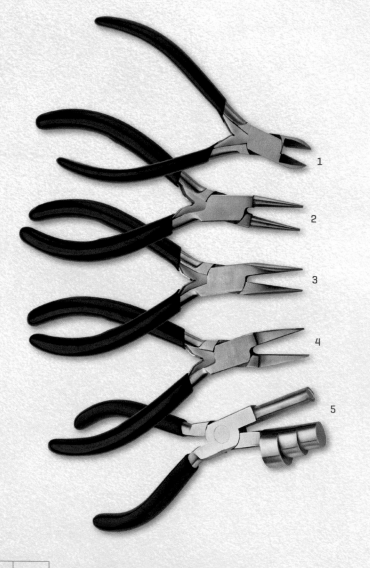

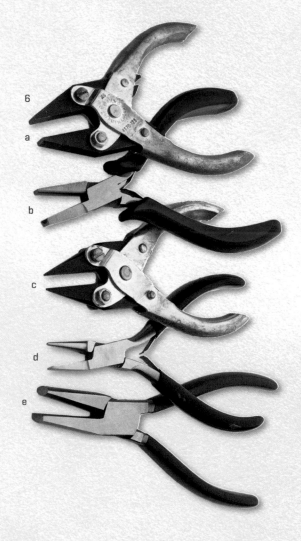

Doming Tools

A DAPPING BLOCK AND PUNCH SET [figure 1] is used to make dome shapes. If you plan on using domed shapes, remember to texture your sheet metal prior to doming. Choose a dapping punch slightly smaller than the dome size. Set your dapping block on a steel work surface before you begin to shape your discs.

Your disc should fit just inside the rim of the dome. Try to position your punch as close to the middle of your disc as possible. If you plan to make your domed disc smaller, continue dapping in successively smaller domes with matching daps. Use a heavy hammer and try to give it a good square whack on the first try. I put an old mouse pad under mine to muffle the sound. Remember that the more you hammer your textured sheet, the more the texture will flatten out. And you'll be hardening your metal at the same time.

I also use the smallest two punches to flare the ends of metal tubing when I'm making tube rivets [see tube riveting in the Techniques section]. I've also used my dapping set to dome brass and copper mesh.

Cutting Tools

Cutting shapes in sheet metal can be achieved with different tools, too. Use a JEWELER'S SAW [figure 2] with proper blades to cut different weights of metal [see blade chart on page 19]. Use this tool for intricate shapes and remember to lubricate your blades often with BUR LIFE. METAL SHEARS [figure 3] are useful, but these Joyce Chen kitchen shears work perfectly well to cut simple shapes in lightweight sheet metal. Use FLUSH CUTTERS [figure 4] to make straight cuts in wire.

DISC CUTTERS [figure 5] are great for making different-sized discs. You'll want to position the punch set over a steel work surface. Use a heavy household hammer if you have one and give it a good whack. Use care with this tool and try to be aware of when you actually punch the disc and stop hammering. You'll save the nice sharp edges of your punches if you don't whack them all the way through to your bench block.

Making Holes

Here is a variety of ways to make holes in your materials. HOLE-PUNCHING PLIERS [figure 1] are an excellent alternative to an expensive flex shaft. The SCREW PUNCH [figure 2] has two sizes built in, and the beauty of these tools is that they're portable. A HAND DRILL [figure 3] requires two hands. Enough said. The DISC CUTTER [figure 4] shown here has a tiny punch that works in a pinch if you need to make a little hole. The hand-held PIN VISE [figure 5] can hold a drill bit, too.

Another nice way to drill holes is with a FLEXIBLE SHAFT DRILL [figure 6]. It isn't an essential tool for making cold-connected jewelry but is a really nice tool to have. I used a cordless drill for the longest time. With a flex shaft, you can swap out bits to handle all types of tasks, from drilling to polishing and everything in between. It has a foot pedal used to control the motor speed. It's meant to hang next to your bench, and after you get one, it quickly becomes your right hand.

Finishing

Finishing with files and sandpaper will reward you with a professional-looking finish and is well worth doing. Use the FILES to round off corners on rough-cut sheet metal. Sand with SANDPAPER in successive grits. The lower the number, the coarser the grit. Start with the lowest number and move up to the highest number [figure 1].

You can make SANDING STICKS [figure 2] with sandpaper and paint stirrers. You'll be reaching for your small set of NEEDLE FILES [figure 3] to flatten the end of your rivet wire, and the round ones are perfect for deburring drill holes. FLEXIBLE SHAFT ACCESSORIES [figure 4] are ideal for polishing and texturing sheet metal. STEEL WOOL [figure 5] and POLISH PADS [figure 6] are a great final step to highlight and bring shine to areas after patination.

LIVER OF SULFUR [figure 7] is used to antique or darken the finish on copper, bronze, and silver. You need only a tiny amount in a large bowl of heated water to achieve many different effects. Use rubber gloves. Warm your metal, dip in the liver of sulfur bath, and quickly quench in cold water.

Dry it off and repeat until you have the effect you desire. Use WOODEN TONGS [figure 8] or RUBBER-TIPPED TONGS to avoid making marks on your jewelry.

If you patina your work, and it's not too fragile, try a TUMBLER [figure 9] for a really nice polished finish. Use one pound of JEWELER'S SHOT [figure 10] in the tumbler with a couple of drops of dish detergent. Fill the tumbler with just enough water to cover the jewelry and the shot. Turn it on for an hour or two, depending on how many pieces and the effect you desire.

Techniques

The following techniques are some of the basics you'll
need in order to get started with the projects in *Metal
Style*. From drilling to sawing and cutting to riveting,
this chapter is designed to give you the skills needed
to get started. The projects include step-by-step
photographs, which are more specific techniques for a
particular project. What you learn here will get you going
on your way to fantastic wearable art!

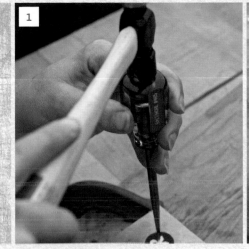

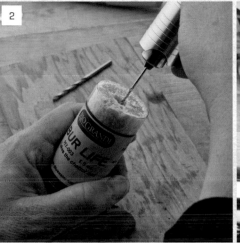

Drilling

TWIST DRILL BIT SIZE	WIRE GAUGE	MM DIAMETER	INCH DIAMETER
#60	18	1.016 mm	.0400"
#55	16	1.321 mm	.0520"
#53	15	1.511 mm	.0595"
#51	14	1.702 mm	.0670"
#46	12	2.057 mm	.0810"
#42	3/32" tubing	2.378 mm	.0935"
#30	1/8" tubing	3.264 mm	.1285"

Use eye protection when you drill metal.

To prepare your site for a drilled hole, first you'll want to dent your metal with a center punch. There are two types of center punches available. The indentation will give your drill bit a seat or nesting place so it won't skid off your mark. To avoid distorting your metal, center punch your metal on a steel work surface. Throughout the projects, we'll refer to this process as center punching [figure 1].

Using a ring clamp to hold sheet metal when drilling is a safe way to hold your work and won't mark the surface of your metal (see the Tools section for ring clamp details). Some common drill bit sizes for common wire gauges are shown in the table at left. Load your drill bit into your drill and always lubricate bits with beeswax or Bur Life [figure 2].

Use a scrap piece of wood as a drilling surface. Position your drill bit on your indentation and make sure you're holding the bit straight up and down. Start the motor slowly and add speed while gently pressing down on the bit to drill the hole. Do not force the drill bit through the metal. Let the drill do the work. The small drill bits will break if you use too much force and if you go too fast. If you need a really large hole, start out with a small bit and successively work into larger bits [figure 3].

There are other ways to make holes in sheet metal. The advantages to using screw punches, disc cutters, and hole-punching pliers are that you don't have to make an initial center punch or dimple in the metal to hold a bit in place.

Sawing and Cutting

Use eye protection when you saw metal.

A jeweler's saw is an essential tool if you plan to cut out custom shapes for your jewelry designs. It takes some time to get used to the fragility of the blades so be prepared to break a few.

It's very important to choose the right blade for your project. Thinner blades will be better for more intricate details. Ideally, 2.5 teeth should come in contact with the edge of your sheet at all times. Suggestions for blade choices based on the gauge (thickness) of your sheet metal are shown in the table at left.

Loading Your Saw Blade

First, you need to load your blade with the teeth positioned in the correct direction and with proper tension to reduce blade breakage.

Loosen both sets of screws. Position the frame (open side faceup) between your body and the edge of your work surface with the handle against your sternum or shoulder. Insert the blade between the top screw pad and the saw frame, with the teeth facing up and toward you. Be careful to position your blade so it's parallel with the spine of your saw frame. Tighten the top screw.

Next you'll want to lean against the frame to create tension while you load the bottom blade. You'll see the frame bend slightly when you lean on it.

Place the bottom blade end between the bottom screw pad and the bottom of the frame while you maintain pressure or tension against the frame and tighten the bottom screw.

When you have the blade loaded, give it a pluck on the back side of the blade. You should hear a high-pitched ping. Take time at this point to make sure the blade is loaded properly. If it isn't, reload it.

Preparing to Cut or Making the First Cut

Run your blade through some beeswax or Bur Life to lubricate it. You'll want to stop and re-lubricate your blade while you work to keep your blade moving freely.

Good posture and positioning helps, too. Sit close to eye level with your work. Brace whatever you are cutting with your non-dominant hand on a scrap piece of wood clamped to your work surface or a bench pin if you have one.

A C-clamp will work to hold the wood to your work surface. If possible, saw out a "V" shape in the front of your scrap.

The V-shape cutout allows more versatility in maneuvering your blade around intricate shapes.

Brace your piece with your nondominant hand on top of your wooden work surface and place the top of your blade against the edge of the piece. Sandwich your blade between your thumb (along the smooth back side of the blade) and the edge of the metal you're cutting to stabilize the blade position.

Swipe the blade UPWARD against your piece using most of the length of your blade. This should chip a tiny groove into your metal to give your blade a stable path to follow on the downward stroke.

SHEET METAL GAUGE	BLADE SIZE
16-gauge sheet metal: #2, 3, 4, or 5 saw blade	18-gauge
18-gauge sheet metal: #1, 1/0, 2, 3, or 4	16-gauge
20-gauge sheet metal: #2/0	15-gauge
24-gauge sheet metal: #5/0, 6/0, 7/0	14-gauge
26-gauge sheet metal: #7/0, 8/0	12-gauge
28-gauge sheet metal: #8/0 or shears	3/32" tubing
30- to 34-gauge sheet metal: cut with shears	1/8" tubing (I use Joyce Chen kitchen shears)

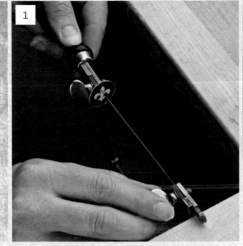

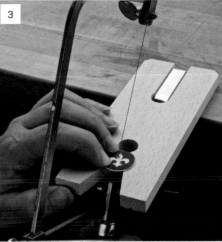

BLADE SIZE	DRILL SIZE FOR PIERCING
8/0	80
7/0	80
6/0	79
5/0	78
4/0	77
3/0	76
2/0	75
1/0	73
1	71
2	70
3	68
4	67
5	65
6	58
7	57
8	55

For the initial pass of the blade, hold your saw frame on a slight angle, with the top of the frame leaning forward. After you have your initial groove, you'll want to straighten out your frame, so the blade is angled only slightly forward. You need to apply a very slight amount of pressure to cut thin sheet metal. Try to saw using most of the length of the blade as you work using long smooth strokes. Be gentle. Breathe. Relax. Hold your frame handle like it's a puppy's leg. Always brace your work against wood and keep your fingers out of the way. Those blades can make nasty cuts in fleshy parts.

Remember to lubricate your blade often and let the blade do the work. You'll be amazed how long they can last if you lubricate them and load them right.

As you come to a corner or sharp angle, saw up and down a few times without any forward pressure while you slowly turn the work and your saw frame. Proceed to saw in a forward motion when the work is facing in the right direction. If your blade becomes snarled, loosen the set screws to try to save your blade. Carefully pull the blade out after you release it from the frame and reload.

If you want to saw out an interior shape, you'll need to drill a hole in your piece and load your blade through the hole [figure 1]. You'll need to make a hole that is large enough to accommodate your saw blade. Depending on the size of the space you have for a drill hole, you might need to figure out what size hole to drill. If you have a huge area to cut out, just grab a drill bit that you know will work. If you have a tight squeeze, there are some suggestions on of drill bit sizes to use and the blade sizes that will fit through those holes in the chart at left. See the drilling section also on page 17 for more information on drilling technique. After you load your piece onto your blade, lubricate your blade with beeswax, Bur Life, or Cut Lube [figure 2].

Brace your work on the bench pin with your nondominant hand, angle your blade forward, and begin to saw out your shape [figure 3].

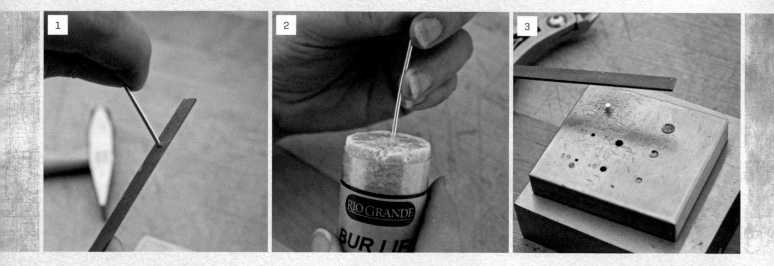

Riveting

TWIST DRILL BIT SIZE	INCHES	WIRE GAUGE	MM DIAMETER
#60	.04"	18	1.016 mm
#55	.05201"	16	1.321 mm
#51	.06701"	14	1.702 mm
#46	.08098"	12	2.057 mm
#51	.0625" (1/16" tubing)	14	1.587 mm
#42	.09375" (3/32" tubing)	11	2.378 mm
#32	.109375" (7/64" tubing)	9	2.778 mm
#30	.125" (1/8" tubing)	8	3.264 mm
#21	.15625" (5/32" tubing)	6	3.969 mm
#10	.1875" (3/16" tubing)	4	4.762 mm

Riveting two pieces of metal together can serve as function and design. Using soft or annealed wire and tubing for rivets is recommended. If the tubing isn't soft, it could split when you're hammering it. For beginners, an 18-gauge wire minimum is recommended.

Wire, screw, and tube gauges should match your drill bit size precisely. A tight fit is essential for riveting success. If you find that your wire or tubing has wiggle room, you'll wind up with a bent rivet and lots of wasted time. Use a smaller drill bit instead of one that you're not sure about, then file the hole with a round file to create a perfect fit.

If you're going to make your own rivets from wire, you'll need to create a "head" on one end of the wire. First, you need to make sure that the end of your wire is flat. Cut a piece of wire with flush cutters and file it just to be sure it's flat [figure 1].

There are different ways to make rivets (almost everyone does it differently). I encourage you to try different techniques to see which way works best for you.

You can either make both rivet heads directly on your piece with a riveting hammer, some wire, and a steel bench block. Or you can make one rivet end head using a vise and finish the other head directly on the piece.

To make both sides of the rivet heads directly on your piece, be sure to start out with a piece of wire that is filed flat on both ends. If it's a decorative rivet (meaning, it does not function) and you're only riveting through one piece of sheet, just drill one hole in the sheet that matches your wire gauge. File the hole with a needle file. Use a riveting hammer and a steel bench block as your work surface. A good rule is to leave one to one and a half times the diameter of the wire above the top and bottom surfaces (a tiny bit). Use the sharp side of the riveting hammer to start tapping lightly on the "head" of the wire, from the center of the "head" in a downward, center-to-outward motion. After two or three taps, flip the piece over and tap two or three times on the other side. Keep flipping and tapping. Try switching to the blunt side of the riveting hammer to shape the head after it starts to flatten out.

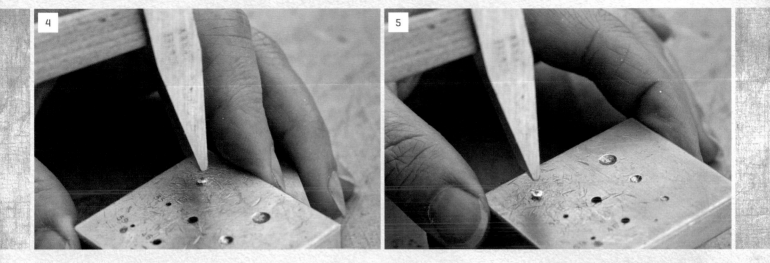

If you have two holes in two pieces of sheet you plan to connect with rivets, drill the holes in the top sheet first, file them, and clamp your two pieces of metal together in a ring clamp. Drill the first hole in the bottom piece using your top piece as a guide. Remove from the ring clamp and rivet. Then clamp the piece again, drill the second hole, and rivet. Finish by drilling and riveting the remaining holes. If you have more than four rivets, rivet the two that are farthest apart first, then rivet with the rest.

You can also use a vise to grip your riveting wire to make your first rivet: The technique is virtually the same. The benefit is that you won't accidentally mar the surface of your work. Clamp the wire in a vise, leaving one to one and a half times the diameter of the wire exposed above the vise jaws. Tap once, dead on, with the rounded side of a ball-peen hammer to flatten the surface. Switch to use the sharp edge of your riveting hammer and use the same downward and outward swiping motion.

When you like the way the wire looks, remove it from the vise. Insert it in the hole and snip the wire to leave the same amount above the surface of your work. One to one and a half times the diameter of the wire is ideal, you

can always trim or file it to the perfect length. If you want to preserve the rounded rivet head, you can create an indentation in your metal work surface somewhere. Then, if you place your rivet head in the indentation, the head will not flatten out as you hammer the opposite side. Work your riveting technique in the same manner as you did for the front, swiping with a riveting hammer in a downward and outward manner.

Here is a brief description of yet another riveting technique. A brass riveting block is a tool created specifically for making wire rivets. Place your riveting block on a flat metal surface. Coat your wire with some Bur Life [figure 2]. Slip your wire into the corresponding gauge hole in the block until it fills the hole [it has markings for commonly used wire gauges]. Use your flush cutters and snip the wire, leaving one to one and a half times the diameter of your wire above the surface of the plate. File the top of the wire flat [figure 3].

Start tapping around the top of the wire. As you tap, turn the plate and tap around the wire with the same riveting motion [figures 4–5]. When you have the desired rivet head, remove the wire from the plate with round-nose pliers or use a piece of the same size wire to push it up from the bottom.

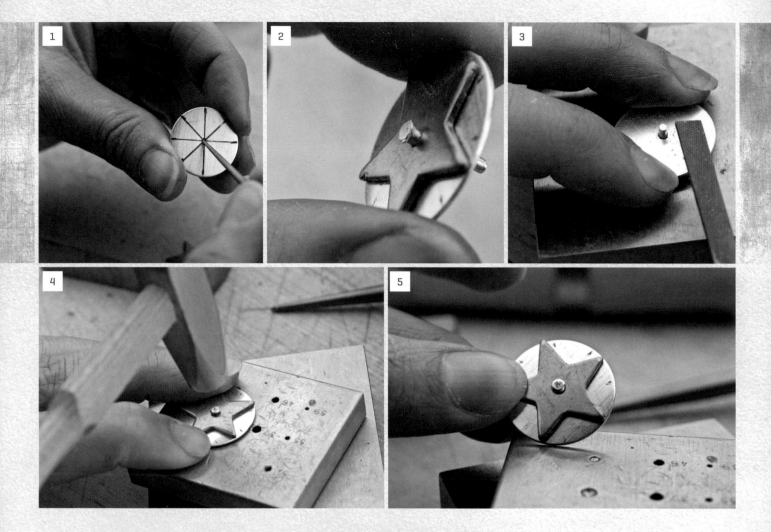

Prepare the pieces you'll be riveting together by drilling and deburring the drilled hole [figure 1]. Insert the rivet through the top of the piece(s) [figure 2]. Snip with flush cutters and file the end flat [figure 3]. The nice thing about the brass riveting block is that it has an indentation formed to protect and shape your rivet head for you while you're riveting the second side. Once you're finished forming the second side, flip the piece over and place the front rivet head in the domed indentation and gently tap the rivet head with the flat side of your riveting hammer to create the same nice rounded head on the back side [figures 4–5].

Rivet heads can be made in a variety of decorative shapes and forms. They must function to hold the pieces together, but beyond that, the head can be used as a decorative element.

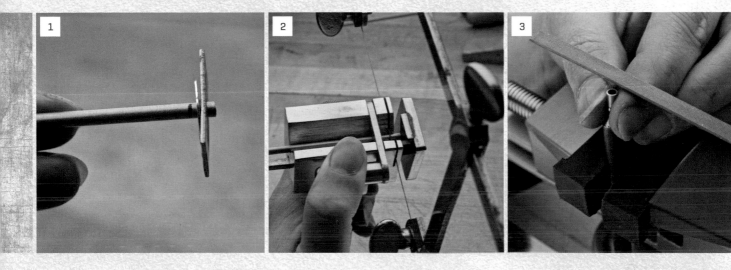

If you make really big rivets with balled up wire, you can stamp a design with a decorative stamp into the head. Janice Berkebile describes how to stamp and texture balled head pins on page 91.

Another type of rivet is a "blind" rivet. These are made to look flush with the finished surface of your work. You'll need to start with a hole, but before you insert your rivet wire, you need to provide a depression or space for the wire to sink down into. You can use a cone shaped burr to create the countersink. Or twist a drill bit in a handheld pin vise that's larger than your hole. You just need to remove enough of the surface of the metal around the hole for the wire to disappear into.

Riveting with tubing or premade eyelets is yet another riveting option. Generally the preferred length for tubing is half the width of the diameter of the tube left above and below the surface.

I use a tube-cutting jig for cutting precise lengths of tubing. Its purpose is to hold your tubing in place with a thumb clamp, and it has a guide for your saw blade so you always make straight cuts on your tubing. It's a great tool for production cutting because the guide is screwed into a fixed position. Thus you wind up with the same length of tubing each time you load it.

With tube rivets, you need to start by figuring out the length of tubing you need. First, file the end of the tubing flat. Then pre-assemble the work onto the tubing to determine the length you'll need and make a cut mark on your tubing with an ultrafine-tip permanent marker [figure 1]. Remove the pieces and lay the tubing in the V-shaped groove of the tube-cutting jig. Loosen the set screw and slide the guide into position so your cut mark lines up with the blade groove. Tighten the guide screw and flip the thumb-keeper over to hold the tubing in place. Lubricate your saw blade and slip it into the blade groove and saw to cut the tubing [figure 2]. File the newly cut end of the tubing flat [figure 3].

Clamp an eyelet setter or a dapping punch in a vise.

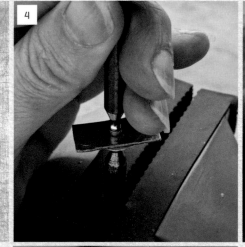

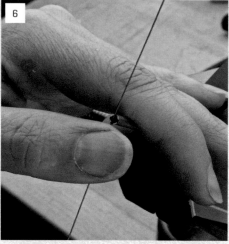

Load your drilled metal pieces on the tubing and on the punch. Use a rawhide mallet and tap the end of another dapping punch to begin flaring out the tubing. You can flare out the tubing any number of ways. I have a "universal eyelet setter" that works well, too, but I prefer to use the rounded-head small punches. You can also do the flip-and-turn technique on a steel surface, with one rounded punch. You just need to flare out the tubing before you start to lay the sides down with a riveting hammer [figure 4].

Lay the piece down on a steel block and use the blunt side of your riveting hammer, using the same technique as you would for wire rivets, flipping it over, and tapping around your tube edge with downward, outward swipes until you have rounded the tubing over all the way around on both sides [figure 5].

There are also decorative variations to tube rivets. I like to slice into my tubing with my jeweler's saw so the cut edges flare out in a cross shape. To do this, make four marks on the end of a full length of tubing. You can also make marks around the diameter of the tubing so you know when to stop sawing. A depth of 2 mm is just right. Load the tubing in a vise and brace your thumb against the back (smooth) side of the blade: swipe UPWARD to start a groove [figure 6]. Saw to your mark, loosen the vise, turn the tubing, slice the other direction, and set the tubing in your tube-cutting jig.

Proceed to cut the length of tubing you need in the jig [figure 7]. Make marks on the new end with permanent marker, hold the tubing with pliers, and slice the tube with your blade [figure 8]. Load the tubing in your hole, use a dapping punch to flare out the top, and flip over to flare out the bottom [figure 9]. Use a riveting hammer to finish flattening out the tubing [figure 10].

If you want to elevate or separate your sheet-metal pieces, or a sheet and a bead, or whatever you choose, you can slip a smaller piece of larger diameter tubing (spacer beads work, too) between your "layers" to make telescoping rivets, which act as a "collar" to separate layers.

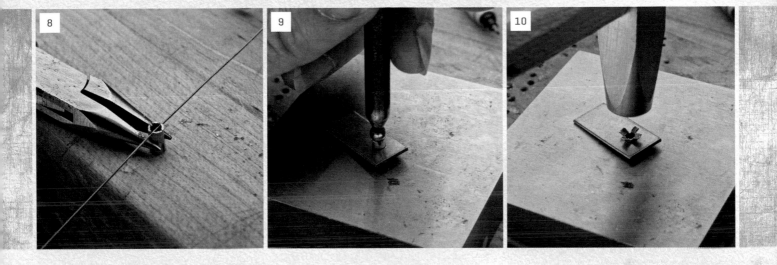

FOUND RIVETS
Nails (copper or brass)
Escutcheon Pins
Electronic Eyelets
Earring Posts
Model Train Parts
Dollhouse Parts
Aeronautics Parts
Industrial or Sewing Grommet

Threaded connectors are easy to use and provide an industrial look. You can use them as you would imagine. They come with a screw, a washer, and a nut. There are different types available: some have a screw top, some are Phillips head, and some are flat with octagonal tops like a bolt. You can use needle-nose pliers to fasten them or use special little wrenches to hold both sides simultaneously while you screw them tight. Simply saw off the ends and rivet them down. Or file them smooth and use a little dab of "lock-tight" on the ends to keep them from unscrewing. Thomas Mann uses threaded connections in his ring project (page 70) and uses a tap to make custom threaded holes.

You can use decorative tab designs to hold or join your work together. They can be as simple as straight tabs or as ornate as you can imagine. You can design your tabs to bend around the object you want to hold in place, and they can go in any direction you choose. You can grip objects from the outside, or they can reach through an interior hole. Just remember to add them to your blank designs when you're drawing your templates.

Staples are a simple way to use metal as another connection. See Connie Fox's work on page 90. She fabricates a "cold-connected staple" by drilling matching sets of holes in her sheet metal layers, she then bends soft wire with pliers to fit in the holes, and then ingeniously rivets the back side to hold them in place. My mind is spinning with ideas just reading about her techniques.

Hinges, adhesives, wire lashing, and epoxy are "cold" connections, too. Endless possibilities really.

Riveted Round-link Chain

DESIGNED BY:
Janice Berkebile

FINISHED SIZE:
10¼" long x 1" wide
(26 cm x 2.5 cm)

I WAS LUCKY ENOUGH TO SEE THE ALEXANDER CALDER jewelry exhibit twice. Seeing his work up close is so inspiring. Knowing something about wirework helped me notice his work in changing planes. I am now exploring changing planes in several applications, and riveting chain is just one of them. Enjoy!

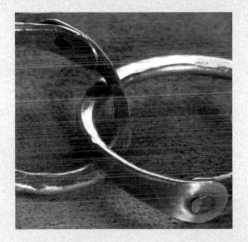

materials

12-gauge sterling silver dead-soft round wire
  (3" or 7.6 cm for each link)
14-gauge copper dead-soft round wire

tools

Large-gauge flush cutters

Chasing hammer

Steel bench block

Flat file or emery board

Ruler

1.8 mm hole-punch pliers

Large (13, 16, and 20 mm) stepped wrap-and-
  tap forming pliers

Riveting stake

Riveting hammer

Mini horn anvil

Chain- or flat-nose pliers

Liver of sulfur

Pro-Polish polishing pad

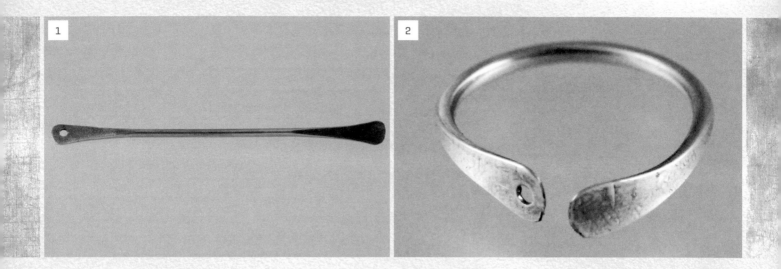

1

2

TIP

Hammer 2 or 3 links at a time, then do another portion of the project to give your arm (elbow) a rest. Remember to slide the link onto the chain you are building unless this is the first link. If you forget, you can connect that riveted link with other chain or use in another project at another time.

1   Cut 3" (7.6 cm) of 12-gauge wire for each link (finished round size is about 25 mm). Flush-cut each end flat.

2   Use a chasing hammer and steel bench block to flatten each end of the wire into a paddle. File any rough edges.

3   Use the hole-punch pliers to punch a hole in the end of both paddles, 1/16" (1.5 mm) from the edge and centered **[figure 1]**.

4   Grasp one of the paddles with the largest (20 mm) step of the stepped pliers. Turn and form half of the wire around the pliers for a loose fit. When the wire becomes difficult to bend, switch to the opposite paddle and bend to form the other side of the link **[figure 2]**.

5   Lay the link flat on the bench block and use a chasing hammer to spread the middle part of the wire flat, perpendicular to the paddle-shaped ends. Use more force with your hammer along the middle of the ring and hammer lightly as you approach the transition in planes **[figure 3]**.

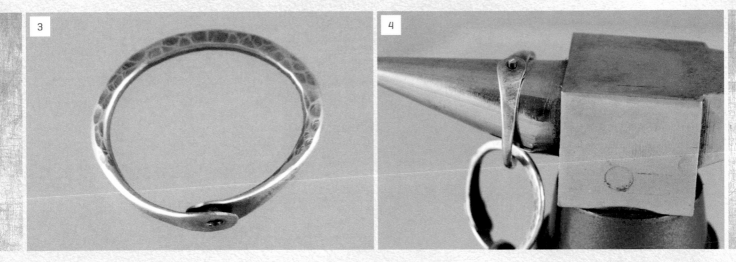

note

The top of the riveting stake has smaller holes than the bottom because they are conical in shape.

6   Cut a length of copper 14-gauge wire about ¼" (6.3 mm) taller than the riveting stake. Put it in the smallest hole that the wire fits in from the top. With the flat side of the riveting hammer, gently start to form a nail head. Once the nail head has been started, pull it out of the stake.

7   Place the link on the mini horn anvil and insert the copper wire through both holes, with the nail head on the inside of the ring.

8   Trim the wire, leaving 1–1.5 mm to form the rivet. Tap around the rim of the copper wire using the sharp side of the riveting hammer and visualizing the edge of the wire rivet. Travel around the outer edge of the wire creating a nail head that helps secure the two ends together.

9   Once a nail head is created, flip your riveting hammer to use the flat side and hammer with increased force to flatten the rivet head **[figure 4]**.

10   Tap all around all the rivet edges, checking with your fingers to make sure all the rivets are smooth.

11   Darken with liver of sulfur. Hand polish with a Pro-Polish pad or tumble to finish.

Starry Night Earrings

DESIGNED BY: **Dawn Bergmaier**

FINISHED SIZE: **1" (2.5 cm) diameter**

THESE EARRINGS WERE INSPIRED BY THE NIGHT SKY, by the glow of the constellations, and the configuration of the stars as seen from the earth.

materials

Two 1¹/₄" (3.1 cm) squares of copper 22-gauge sheet

Two 2" (5 cm) pieces of sterling silver 20-gauge round wire

Colored epoxy resin

tools

Fine-tip permanent marker

Disc cutter

Brass mallet or steel hammer

Drill or flex shaft

Drill bits: #54 and #65

Dapping block and punches

Rawhide or plastic mallet

Polishing machine

Tripoli polish

Rouge polish

Liver of sulfur

Brass wire brush

Round-nose pliers

Silly Putty

Smooth round object (small glass vase or an egg)

Wire cutters

Polishing cloth

Rotary tumbler with stainless-steel shot and burnishing compound *(optional)*

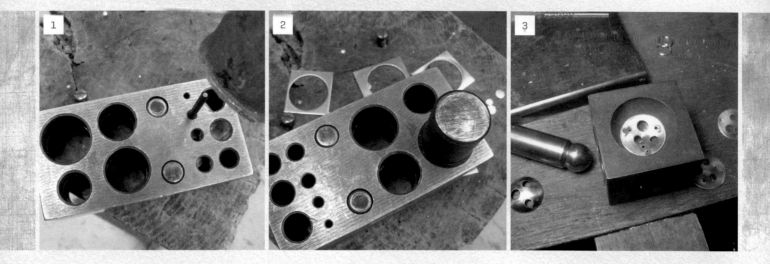

1 Draw two 1" (2.5 cm) circles on the copper sheet using the 1" (2.5 cm) hole in the disc cutter as a template.

2 Use the disc cutter to punch two ³⁄₁₆" (4.7mm) discs and one ¼" (6.3mm) disc out of the center of each drawn circle [figure 1].

3 Line up the drawn circle outline in the 1" (2.5cm) disc cutter hole and punch out a 1" (2.5cm) disc; repeat for the other circle outline [figure 2].

4 Use a #65 drill bit to drill 1 hole in the top of each disc for the 20-gauge ear wire. Drill each disc with 3 more randomly placed holes: 2 with a #54 drill bit and 1 with a #65 drill bit.

5 Use a large dapping punch and rawhide mallet to dome the discs in a dapping block [figure 3].

6 Polish the domed discs with Tripoli and rouge.

TIP

Use a brass mallet instead of a steel hammer with your disc cutter, if you have one. The brass absorbs the vibrations of the strike and extends the life of the cutting punches.

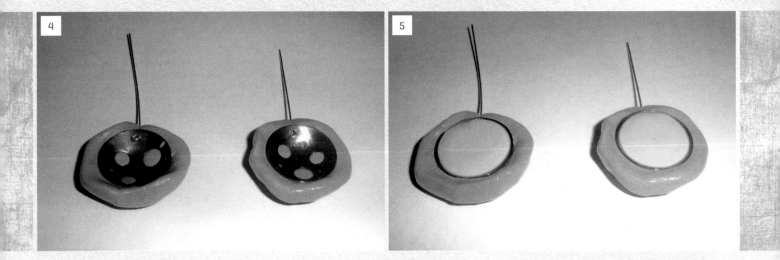

To get an even finish, allow the pieces to rest in the liver of sulfur solution for one minute, then remove and scrub lightly with a soapy brass wire brush. Rinse with water and return to liver of sulfur solution. Repeat three or four times to get an even patina with a low sheen.

note

The Silly Putty will push through the cutout holes a bit, giving the resin a nice concave appearance in the finished earrings.

7   Patina the discs and the 20-gauge sterling silver wire in a hot liver of sulfur solution.

8   Use round-nose pliers to bend small "stopper loops" at one end of each silver wire.

9   Form Silly Putty into bowl shapes with a smooth rounded object; try a small glass vase or egg. Otherwise, the Silly Putty and the epoxy resin will pick up your fingerprints [figure 4].

10   Insert the ear wires through the earring holes with the end loops acting as stoppers inside the domed discs.

11   Press the discs into the Silly Putty.

12   Follow the mixing directions for the epoxy. I mixed a golden yellow color. Fill the domed earrings with the epoxy resin. Allow the resin to fully cure before removing the earrings from the Silly Putty [figure 5].

13   Remove the earrings from the Silly Putty. Trim and shape the ear wires and give them a brief final polish with a polishing cloth.

Garden Wind Gong Pendant

DESIGNED BY: Dawn Bergmaier

FINISHED SIZE:
1⁹/₁₆" wide x 1¾" high
(4 cm x 4.45 cm)

THIS PENDANT WAS INSPIRED by the Asian musical gong instrument, which is played with a large soft mallet and can be found hanging from a tree branch in a garden.

materials

2" x 2½" (5 x 6.3 cm) of brass 20-gauge sheet
2" x 2½" (5 x 6.3 cm) of copper 18- or
    20-gauge sheet
1½" (3.8 cm) of brass 8-gauge wire
2 sterling silver 2" (5 cm) 20-gauge head pins

tools

White paper
Permanent markers: fine and extrafine points
Carbon paper
Masking tape
Ballpoint pen
Ruler
Jeweler's saw frame
#1 saw blades
Lubricant or beeswax
Sandpaper: various grits
Rubbing alcohol
Newspapers
Nitrile gloves
Safety glasses
Apron
Ferric chloride

Glass dish or disposable plastic container
Scrap brass
Baking soda
Water
Tongs
Toothbrush
Powdered pumice
Brass brush
Files: hand and needle
Assorted hammers
Steel bench block
Center punch
Drill or flex shaft
#65 drill bit
Mallet
Mushroom stake
Round-nose pliers
Parallel pliers
Tripoli polish
Rouge polish
Chain-nose pliers
Liver of sulfur
Rouge cloth
Thin flat piece of wood
Polishing machine with buffs

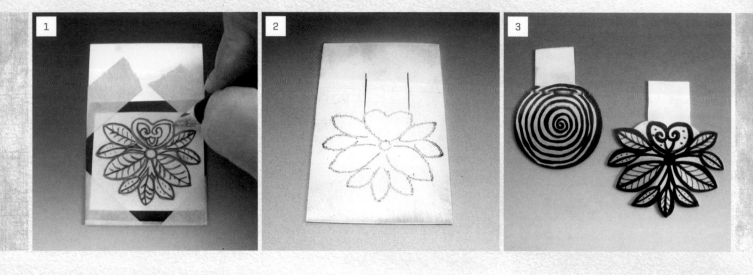

1. Draw a design on paper that fits the brass 20-gauge sheet. Be sure to draw a ⅝" x ⅝" (1.5 x 1.5 cm) tab as part of the design, for the hinges. Place a small piece of carbon paper (carbon side down) on the brass and place your drawing on top. Tape the pieces in place. Trace the design, pressing firmly with a ballpoint pen, and the carbon paper will transfer the design onto the brass [figures 1 and 2].

2. Use a permanent marker to draw a 1½" (3.8 cm) circle with a ⅝" x ⅝" (1.5 x 1.5 cm) tab on copper 20-gauge sheet. Saw out the shapes with the jeweler's saw frame and #1 saw blade. Lightly sand the surfaces of the metal pieces and then wipe them with rubbing alcohol to be sure they are clean; residue resists the etching process.

3. Use a permanent fine-point and an extrafine-point marker for 2 different line weights. Draw the images onto the metal freehand, or use the same carbon paper transfer technique described earlier, and draw over the carbon lines with the permanent marker. I have also drawn the word "GROW" on the back of the copper piece [figure 3].

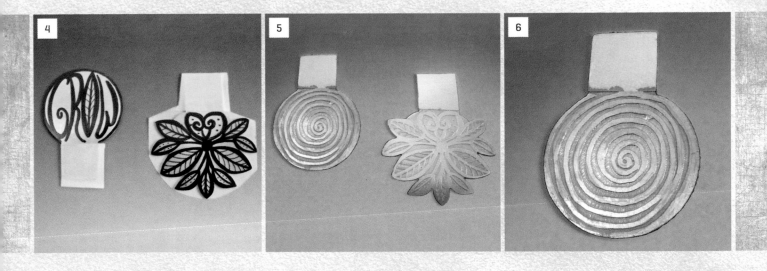

notes

Ferric chloride will stain anything it comes in contact with.

A batch of ferric chloride is good for about 5 hours of etching. When finished, neutralize with a baking soda and water solution (2 cups water and ¼ cup baking soda). Dispose at the nearest hazardous-waste disposal site.

TIP

Be careful not to etch right through the metal.

4 Cover the hinge metal with masking tape to protect it from the etching solution. Cover the back of the brass leaf piece with masking tape. Since both sides of the copper piece will be etched, you do not need to cover the back side **[figure 4]**.

5 Etching: Cover your work area with newspapers. Wear nitrile gloves, safety glasses, and an apron. Have proper ventilation and do not inhale the vapors. Pour enough ferric chloride into a glass dish or disposable plastic container to cover your pieces. Prop up the two-sided copper piece on a bent piece of scrap brass. This will allow the ferric chloride to etch both sides at the same time. Place the leafy brass piece faceup, next to the copper piece. Bathe the pieces in the etching solution for about an hour and a half. The permanent marker will not hold up to the ferric chloride for longer than that, so if you want to etch deeper, you will need to reapply your drawing **[figure 5 (front) and figure 6 (back)]**.

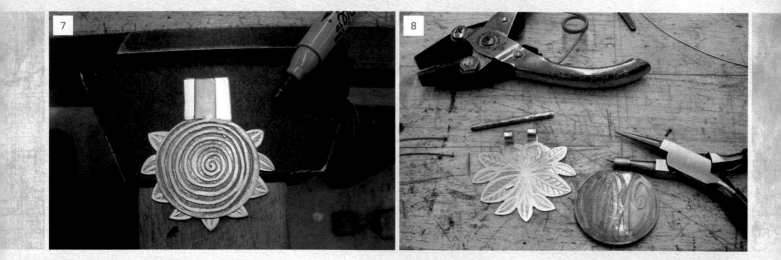

6 Use tongs to take the metal out of the ferric chloride, put it into a bath of baking soda and water to neutralize the etching solution and halt the process. Rinse with water and scrub with a toothbrush and powdered pumice to remove the marker lines. Finish by scrubbing the pieces with a wet, soapy brass wire brush to give the pieces a little shine.

7 File and sand the edges of the metal pieces.

8 Place the pieces on top of each other and mark the copper metal tab for the center hinge. Make it ¼" wide by ⅝" (6.3 mm x 1.5 cm). The center hinge will be wider than the outer brass ones. Cut the copper with the jeweler's saw, sand, and file.

9 Place the copper piece on top of the brass piece and use it as a template to mark the edges of the outer brass hinges [figure 7].

10 Cut the 2 brass hinges straight and parallel to measure about ⅛" wide and ⅝" (3.1 mm x 1.5 cm) long. Check for a snug fit on either side of the center copper hinge strip. File and sand the edges.

11 Hammer the 1½" (3.8 cm) piece of brass 8-gauge wire (rod) with various hammers on a steel bench block to give it a rough and rugged texture. Copper would also work well for this piece since it would pick up the patina nicely.

12 Mark 2 hole locations on the brass rod ⅜" (9.5 mm) from the center on both sides. Center punch and drill holes with a #65 drill bit.

13 Use a mallet and mushroom stake to slightly dome the copper piece.

14 Use round-nose and parallel pliers to form the metal tabs into hinges to fit around the hammered brass rod [figure 8].

TIP

I rolled the copper hinge backward and the brass hinges forward.

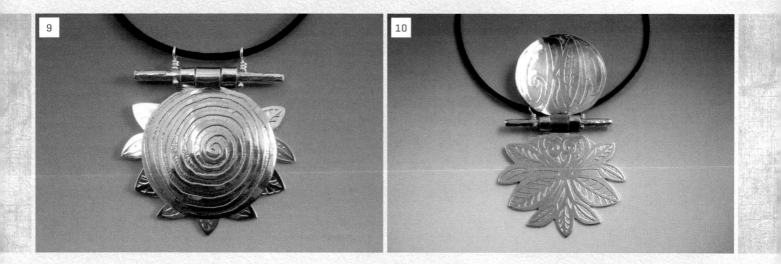

15　Pre-polish the three pieces with Tripoli and then finish polish with rouge.

16　Put the rod through the hinges and lock it into place by feeding the 20-gauge wire through the 2 drilled holes and creating a wire-wrapped loop on top. I used some sterling silver wire that was balled on one end. Premade thick wire head pins will work just as well [figure 9 (closed) and figure 10 (open)].

17　At this point, you can stop and have a nice highly polished finished piece. Or you can continue with patina to add a little more contrast and age to the piece.

18　Submerse the piece in a hot liver of sulfur solution for five to ten minutes to darken. The copper will blacken, and while the brass usually doesn't change much, I got some greens showing up that I liked and wanted to try to keep in the recesses.

19　Rub the patina off the high areas and polish at the same time by wrapping a rouge cloth over a thin flat piece of wood (sanding stick). This lets the patina stay dark and matte in the recesses. Wrap the cloth around your thumb to polish the inside concave area that says "GROW." Clean the rouge off with the yellow side of the cloth.

20　Finish with a chain, piece of cord, or leather through the wire loops.

Medallion Bracelet

DESIGNED BY:
Karen Dougherty

FINISHED SIZE:
2³/₄" wide x 1¼" high
(7 cm x 3.18 cm)

MY GOAL FOR THIS JEWELRY PROJECT was to use an "end" piece of screening that I found with a pretty frilly edge. It was the end of the roll, and I thought it was really great looking. I also wanted to create a unique clasping mechanism.

materials

Sterling silver 24-gauge sheet

Manufactured metal blank shapes.

- Sterling silver 10-gauge round: one 1¼" (3.1cm)
- Sterling silver 22-gauge round: one ³/₄" (1.9cm), two ½" (1.2cm)

2 copper 17mm flower shapes

2 sterling silver flower spacers that fit ³/₃₂" (2.3 mm) tubing

³/₈" x 5" (9.5 mm x 12.7 cm) of 40x40 threads-per-inch brass screening (edge piece)

8 pieces of 1" (2.5 cm) scrap wire

Sterling silver 22-gauge wire

10" (25.4 cm) of sterling silver dead-soft 14-gauge wire

1" (2.5 cm) of copper ³/₃₂" (2.3 mm) tubing

1" (2.5 cm) of copper ¹/₈" (3.1 mm) tubing

4" (10.1 cm) of sterling silver 7mm cable chain

3½" (8.8 cm) of sterling silver 5mm rolo chain

tools

Dot-pattern texture hammer

Steel bench block

Circle template

Fine-tip permanent marker

Ruler

Center punch

Flex shaft

Drill bits: #42 and #51

Round needle file

Doming block and punch

Flush cutters

Riveting hammer

Brass riveting block

Disc cutter

Design stamps

Jeweler's saw frame

#2/0 saw blades

2 pairs of chain-nose pliers

Needle-nose pliers

Round-nose pliers

Liver of sulfur

Pro-Polish polishing pad

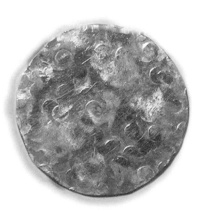

1

2

1 Using the dot-pattern hammer, texture the 1¼" (3.1cm) disc on both sides and the ¾" (1.9cm) disc on one side **[figure 1]**.

2 Using the fine-tip permanent marker and the circle template as a guide, mark 8 equidistant dots on the 1¼" (3.1cm) disc, ⅛" (3.2mm) inside the edge. Mark the center of both discs by drawing 3 equidistant lines across the face of the metal; where they meet is the center.

3 Center punch and drill all the marked dots in both discs with a #51 drill bit. Use a round needle file to ream the holes smooth.

4 Create a dome shape in the ¾" (19mm) disc with the punch and 1" dome in the doming block.

5 Cut a ⅜" x 5" (9.5 mm x 12.7 cm) piece of screening.

6 Form the screening around the edge of the large disc, using eight 1" (2.5 cm) pieces of scrap wire to hold the screening in place as you form it. Line up the mesh so that the outer loops will fall just inside the edge of the disc. Visualize the holes on the base disc through the mesh and use a round needle file to poke holes through the mesh, inserting scrap wire as you go to hold the mesh in place. Continue forming the screening around the diameter, inserting the scrap wires. Snip the mesh with flush cutters as you go, allowing the mesh to overlap where it folds or kinks. Be careful not to snip too close to the looped part of the mesh. Allow an overlap of about ⅛" (3.1 mm) at the end and trim the excess screening **[figure 2]**.

TIP

To find the correct punch for the dome, the punch should fit precisely into the dome, before you insert your disc. If your disc fits just inside the rim of the dome, you have chosen the right size dome.

TIP

If you don't have an end piece, cut a 1" (2.5 cm) circle of screening with the disc cutter and decorate the edge with wire.

TIP

I used the brass riveting block for nice round rivet heads.

note

The cable chain should fit comfortably between the two pieces, but it should be a tight fit in the space; this space will act as part of the clasping mechanism.

7   Remove 1 wire at a time and rivet every other hole with a piece of sterling silver 14-gauge wire **[figure 3]**.

8   Use the disc cutter to punch a ¼" (6.3mm) disc from the sterling silver 24-gauge sheet. Texture the disc on one side with the design stamps. Center punch and drill a hole with a #51 drill bit in the center. This will be the spacer on the top of the bracelet medallion.

9   Using the jeweler's saw frame and #2/0 saw blade, saw a 5 mm length of ⁹⁄₃₂" (2.3 mm) copper tubing and file the ends flat. Cut a ¼" (6.3 mm) piece of sterling silver 14-gauge wire with flush cutters and file the ends flat. Insert the wire through the top spacer, the domed disc, the copper tubing, and the large disc. Rivet both sides of the wire.

10   Remove 4 links from the cable chain and attach one to each of the open holes on the large disc **[figure 4]**.

11   Texture 2 copper flower shapes on both sides with the dot-pattern texture hammer. Eyeball to find the center and center punch. Drill the center hole with a #42 drill bit. Drill 1 more hole just inside the petal shape ⅛" (3.1 mm) from the edge.

12   Texture one side of each of the sterling silver ½" (1.2cm) discs with the dot-pattern texture hammer. Mark the centers, center punch, and drill the center holes with a #42 drill bit. Place 1 disc texture-side down into a ⅝" (1.5 cm) dome and hammer the matching dapping punch, then repeat in a smaller ½" (1.2 cm) dome; repeat for the other disc.

13   Thread 1 flower shape and 1 domed silver disc onto a piece of ³⁄₃₂" (2.3 mm) tubing. Using the cable chain as a guide, separate the copper flower and the domed silver disc, leaving just space enough to accommodate the width of the cable chain. Make 2 marks on the tubing to determine the length of the "collar" piece of tubing needed to act as the spacer between the dome and the flower shape. I needed a ¼" (6.3 mm) piece of ⅛" (3.1 mm) round copper tubing for each clasp.

14 Cut two ¼" (6.3 mm) pieces of ⅛" (3.1 mm) copper tubing and file the ends flat. Set aside.

15 Hold one length of ³⁄₃₂" (2.3 mm) copper tubing and make a mark with the permanent marker ³⁄₃₂" (2.3 mm) from the end, all the way around the tube. Mark 4 equidistant points on the end of the tubing as a guide for sawing. Using the jeweler's saw and #2/0 saw blade, saw along the crosshatch marks down to the line around the circumference of the tube. Using round-nose pliers, bend the split sections of tubing into a loop that touches the base of the tubing. Thread 1 silver spacer bead, 1 domed disc, one ⅛" (3.1 mm) tube spacer, and 1 flower disc onto the ³⁄₃₂" (2.3 mm) tubing. Repeat this step for the other clasp.

16 Push all the components to the split end of the tubing and mark the tubing for your final cut, leaving 1 mm on the end for the rivet. Remove all the pieces, cut the tubing with the jeweler's saw frame and #2/0 saw blade. Add the components back onto the tubing.

17 To make the bottom of the rivet, try using the doming block. I stood my pieces upside down in a small dome in my doming block, and it worked really nicely to curve over the top of the rivet into a nice even shape. Rivet each set.

18 Patina all of the components and chain with liver of sulfur; rinse and dry. Polish with a Pro-Polish pad.

19 Cut a 3½" (8.8 cm) length of rolo chain. Attach both ends of the chain to the holes in the flower components of the clasp using sterling silver 22-gauge wire and wrapped loops.

20 Hold the bracelet together on your wrist to measure the length of cable chain needed on each side of the medallion, to attach the medallion to the clasp components. I attached 9 links on one side and 8 on the other [figures 5 and 6].

TIP

One side should have one extra link to help clasp and unclasp the bracelet.

Doming Metal

Use a dapping block and punches to make domed effects in your jewelry designs. There are a few things to keep in mind when you're doming metal. Reverse this technique for a textured side up cup shape.

1 When possible, work with annealed or soft metal.

2 Use a large leather hammer for best results, if you have one, and try to get your dome to form with one forceful blow of the hammer.

3 Drill your holes before you punch. They will distort slightly, so it's a good idea to drill them a bit smaller and file them round or ream them out after you've completed the doming process.

4 For precision domes, start with a punch that measures slightly smaller than your die (or dome) shape. Successively punch your metal with larger punches to achieve the desired dome shape.

5 If you're doming textured metal, it will flatten out a bit as you work it into a domed shape. If you're texturing the metal yourself, you might want to create deep textures, to allow for the flattening effect. Also keep in mind that you need to put the textured side of the disc facedown into your die if you want your texture on the outside of the dome.

ALSO USED IN:

Starry Night Earrings, page 030
Riveted Flower Rings, page 126

Fold-formed Leaf Bracelet

DESIGNED BY:
Marthe Roberts-Shea

FINISHED SIZE:
Open: 6" long x 1¼" wide
(15.2 cm x 3.18 cm)
Closed: 2½" diameter x 1¼" high
(6.35 cm x 3.18 cm)

I AM CONTINUALLY AMAZED by the limitless possibilities of fold-forming. From the technique's curving, ruffled, and organic results—this bracelet was born. The metal is work-hardened throughout its fabrication. It is a lot lighter than it appears. I love the idea of a large metal presence without the weight of heavier metal.

materials

2½" x 3" (6.3 x 7.6 cm) of sterling silver
26-gauge sheet

1½" x 1½" (3.8 x 3.8 cm) of copper 20-gauge
sheet

1½" x 1½" (3.8 x 3.8 cm) of NuGold 20-gauge
sheet

8" (20.3 cm) of sterling silver 18-gauge wire

6" (15.2 cm) of copper 18-gauge wire
[optional]

6" (15.2 cm) of brass 18-gauge wire [optional]

6" (15.2 cm) of sterling silver 14-gauge
rectangle wire

2 sterling silver grooved 12mm rings

tools

Fine-tip permanent marker

Vise

Plastic ruler or scraper

Assorted forging hammers

2" x 4" (5 x 10.1 cm) pine wood block, 7–8"
(17.7–20.3 cm) long

Forming hammer

12 mm goldsmith's hammer

Steel bench block

Metal scribe

Flex shaft

#60 drill bit

Jeweler's saw frame

#2 saw blades

Half-round file, #2 cut

Assorted needle files

Bracelet mandrel

Rawhide mallet

3/16" (4.7 mm) disc cutter

Long-nose pliers

Draw tongs

Flush cutters

Small horn anvil

Riveting hammer

Half-round pliers

3/16" (4.7 mm) mandrel or round bezel mandrel

Parallel pliers

2400-grit sandpaper

Cratex or Advantedge wheels or bits

Plastic or wooden toaster tongs

Liver of sulfur

#000 steel wool or soft brass brush

Polishing compound

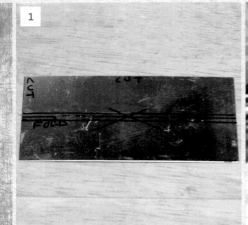

1 Bracelet Segments: Cut two 1¼" x 3" [3.1 x 7.6 cm] pieces of sterling silver 26-gauge sheet. Use the permanent marker to draw a horizontal line across the 3" length of each sheet. Draw dotted lines ⅛" above and below the center line. The solid line is where the fold will be. The dotted lines are placement guides for vise positioning **[figure 1]**.

2 Using your hands, fold one sheet in half with the drawn lines facing out. Place the sheet in the vise, aligning the dotted lines to the top of the vise jaws. Tighten the vise as far as it will go. This will crease the fold line of the metal. Use a plastic scraper, or any pry tool, to pry the sides until both sides of the fold are flat against the vise. Use a forging hammer to flatten both sides of the metal **[figure 2]**.

3 Remove the piece from the vise and turn it over. You should have a pronounced horizontal folded seam across the metal.

4 Secure the wood block in the vise. Use the forming hammer to pound a substantial indent into the wood. Placement of the indent should be off-center and very close to one edge of the block. You will use this indent to "ruffle" the metal **[figure 3]**.

5 With the pronounced seam facing up, place one side of the metal on the wood block. Use the forming hammer to contour the metal into the wood's indentation **[figure 4]**.

Next, position the metal so that part of it is hanging off the edge of the wood block. Resting the metal over the edge of the block and hammering, just below it, off the block, will produce a "peak" in the metal. A "valley" will be formed where you hammered just below the wood. Continue hammering until you get the desired "ruffling" effect **[figure 5]**.

6 Use the goldsmith's hammer and a small steel forming block to texture the leaf's center vein. Flatten about ¼" [6.3 mm] of the vein on both ends of the leaf. Use the scribe to make a divot where you are going to drill a rivet hole. Use the #60 drill bit to drill one rivet hole in the end of each leaf shape **[figure 6]**.

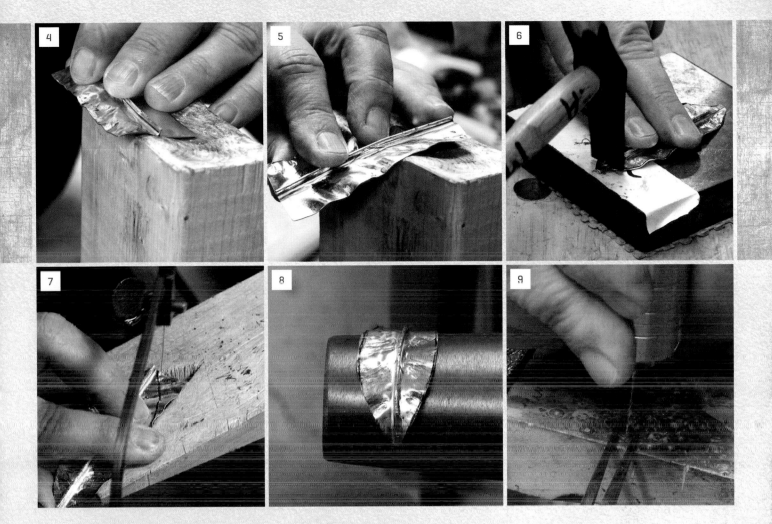

It's difficult to hold a tiny metal dot in place while you drill. To stabilize the dots, hold them in place with a long-nose pair of pliers. It also makes it easier to pick up the dots after they have been drilled.

7   Draw a leaf shape on the ruffled silver. Use the jeweler's saw and #2 saw blade to cut around the shape that you have drawn. File the edges of the cut leaf shape [figure 7].

8   Contour the leaf over a round bracelet mandrel with a rawhide mallet [figure 8].

9   Use a ³/₁₆" (4.7 mm) hole cutter to punch dots out of copper and NuGold sheet. Scribe a divot in the center of each dot.

10 Place the drill bit in the divot and drill a rivet hole with a #60 drill bit in each dot [figure 9].

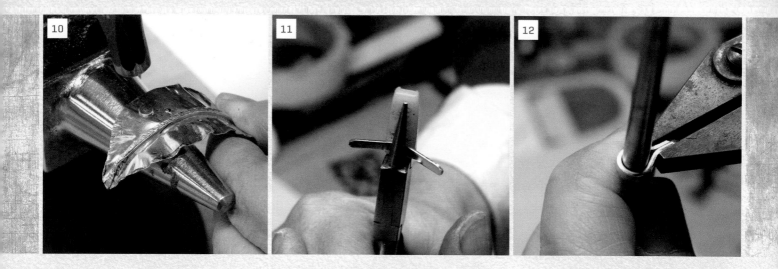

11 Use the permanent marker to mark where you want the dot locations on the bracelet leaves. Scribe a divot and drill with a #60 bit where you have marked. Place one end of the 18-gauge wire in the draw tongs and the other end in the vise. Pull with the tongs until the wire is straightened. Thread the 18-gauge wire through one hole and through a dot. Cut the wire with a flush cutter, leaving ¹⁄₁₆" (1.5 mm) of wire above and below the leaf. File the rivet top and bottom so that each end is flat. Rivet using a small horn anvil and riveting hammer. Use a wire color that is in contrast to the color dot you choose. Continue riveting until all of the dots are in place [figure 10].

12 Cut three 1¼" (3.1 cm) pieces of rectangle wire for the hinges. Cut one 1½" (3.8 cm) piece of rectangle wire for the hook. Texture if desired and round the ends of each piece with the file.

13 Take one of the 1¼" (3.1 cm) wire pieces and using half-round pliers, bend the wire to start forming a long "U" [figure 11].

14 Slip the U-shaped piece on a ³⁄₁₆" (4.7 mm) mandrel or bezel mandrel and use parallel pliers to flatten part of the "U" ends. Continue this process for the other 2 "U" pieces. If you have done this correctly—the "U" wire is now shaped like a loop. Pattern the loop on the mandrel with the goldsmith's hammer if desired [figures 12–13].

15 Using the half-round pliers, bend the 1½" (3.8 cm) wire to form a rounded "L". Bend one tip of the wire so that it flares up.

16 Scribe a divot and drill 1 rivet hole in the end of the "L" wire and 1 rivet hole through the flattened part of each loop; use a #60 drill bit for both [figure 14].

17 Thread 1 of the 12mm grooved rings through 1 of the loops and "sandwich" one leaf end between the flattened ends of the loop making sure that all the holes that you drilled line up. Thread 18-gauge silver wire into the top hole of the loop through the leaf and through to the other side. Be sure to leave ¹⁄₁₆" (1.5 mm) of wire above and below the surfaces of the leaf. Rivet in place [figure 15].

18 Thread another loop through the 12mm grooved ring that you have already attached to 1 leaf and rivet. The result should be 2 leaves connected by a loop, a 12mm grooved ring, and another loop. Repeat one more time to attach the end loop.

TIP

Before you finish riveting, check to see that the loop is in line with the hammered vein of the leaf. If you wait until the loop is totally riveted down—the connection might be so tight that you might not be able to pivot it.

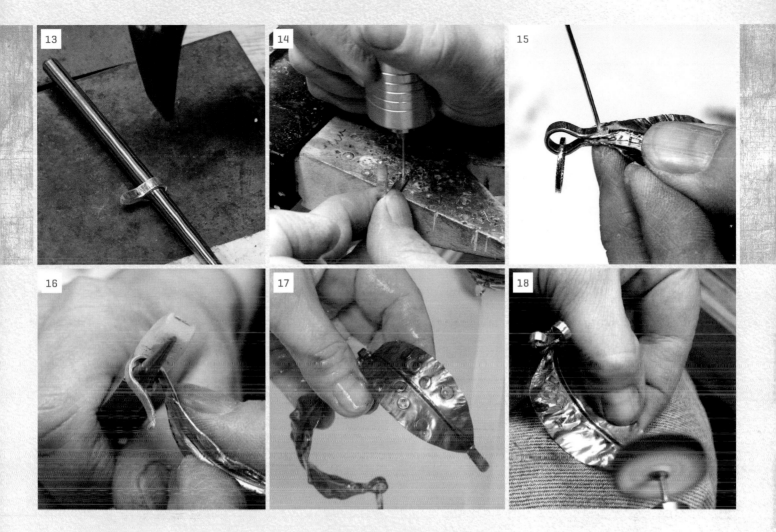

19 Turn the bracelet over and line up the remaining leaf rivet hole and the "L" hook hole. The bent end of the wire should be pointing toward the floor. Rivet the "L" in place.

20 Bend the "L" with half-round pliers until the flared end is almost touching the bracelet. Leave a little space between the bracelet and the hook so that the 12mm grooved ring can slide through [figure 16].

21 File and sand with 2400-grit sandpaper to smooth all the rough edges. Use a flex shaft with Advantege or Cratex wheels to further smooth all the edges.

22 Use plastic or toaster tongs to dip the bracelet in liver of sulfur. Rinse with water and dry [figure 17].

23 Brush with steel wool or a soft brass brush to highlight the patina.

24 Polish the back of the bracelet to a high shine with polishing compound and flex shaft bit [figure 18].

Free-spirit Brooch

DESIGNED BY:
Julie Sanford

FINISHED SIZE:
**1½" wide x 1¼" high
(3.8 x 3.1 cm)**

THE SUBJECT OF FREE SPIRIT comes up in my work often and originates from a snorkeling encounter I had with a young sea turtle. I was thrilled and surprised to see this little turtle and followed him for some time. Create delightful depth and dimension with this three-layer pierced, stacked, and riveted brooch.

materials

1¼" x 1½" (3.1 x 3.8 cm) of copper 20–22-gauge sheet

1¼" x 1½" (3.1 x 3.8 cm) of copper/brass mokume gane 20–22-gauge sheet

1¼" x 1½" (3.1 x 3.8 cm) of sterling silver 20–22-gauge sheet

8" (20.3 cm) of copper 16-gauge wire

8 sterling silver 2x2mm crimp tubes

tools

Sandpaper: 400- and 600-grit

Fine-tip permanent marker

Flex shaft or drill

1/16" (1.5 mm) drill bit

Jeweler's saw frame

#2 saw blades

Wax

Needle files

Dapping block and punch

Anvil

Plastic mallet

Wire cutters

Round-nose pliers

Flat-nose pliers

Needle nose pliers

Buffing wheel/compound

Liver of sulfur

Wax sealer

Covered plastic container

Ammonia and salt

Clear matte acrylic spray

Small bench vise

Small ball-peen hammer

Masking tape

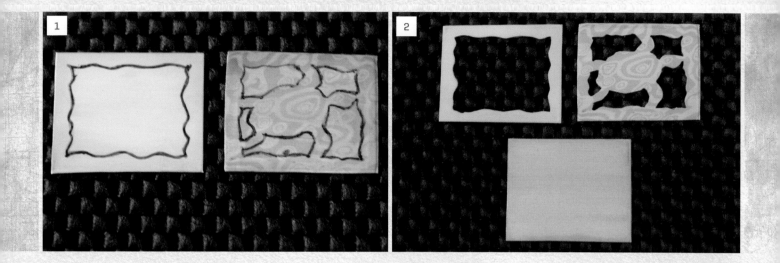

1. Prepare the metal by sanding the surfaces and edges to 600-grit. Depending on the condition of your sheet you may need to start with a coarser grit and work progressively down to 600-grit. The surfaces should appear uniformly smooth and free of scratches and abrasions. Draw or transfer the template for the frame onto the sterling silver sheet and the template for the turtle onto the mokume gane sheet [figure 1].

2. Drill pilot holes and cut out the negative areas with a jeweler's saw frame and #2 saw blade. File the inside edges smooth [figure 2].

3. To add dimension and contrast, patina the turtle sheet with liver of sulfur, then lightly dome the center of the piece with a dapping block and punch. Straighten the frame with a flat anvil and plastic mallet [figure 3].

4. Drill 1/16" (1.5 mm) rivet holes in the corners of the frame. Using the holes in the frame as a guide, mark the same hole placement on the turtle sheet and copper sheet with the permanent marker; drill the holes. Mark and drill 2 more holes on the upper half of the copper sheet, spaced about 2" (5 cm) apart, to accommodate the pin stem mechanism [figure 4].

5. To make the pin mechanism, use 5" (12.7 cm) of 16-gauge wire and round-nose pliers. Form 1 complete loop in the center of the wire. Insert the wire into the copper sheet so the coil is on the back of the sheet. Bring the inserted end of the wire up through the second hole. It should look like a staple on the front side [figure 5].

6. To tighten the pin mechanism to the sheet and create a catch for the pin stem, make a loop with the short wire, keeping it flush to the sheet. Gently tighten/hammer the loop flat with a plastic mallet. With flat-nose pliers, bend the tail end of the wire perpendicular to sheet. File the end of the wire smooth [figures 6, 7, and 8].

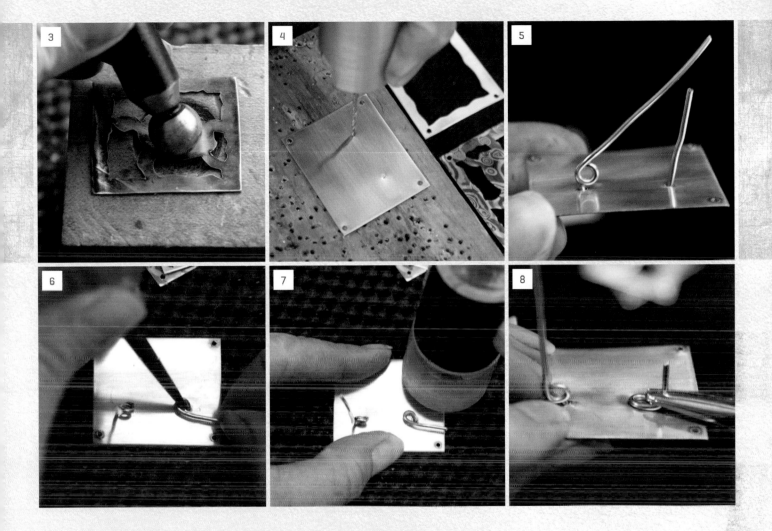

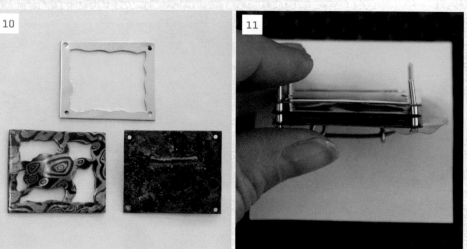

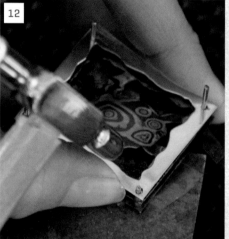

7 Bend the pin stem wire down to meet the catch wire. Trim the stem, leaving ⅛" (3.1 mm) beyond the catch. File the stem to a point and smooth with sandpaper to a fine grit. Use round-nose pliers to bend the catch wire over, to provide the hook/catch for the stem [figure 9].

8 Prepare all pieces for final assembly. File, sand, polish, and patina all three sheets to the desired finishes. For this project, the frame was finished to a high polish, the turtle sheet was patinaed with liver of sulfur, then a wax sealer was added, and the copper sheet was patinaed using ammonia and salt with a clear matte acrylic spray added for the finish.

9 Use 3" (7.6 cm) of sterling silver 16-gauge wire to begin a rivet. Secure the wire in a small bench vise, leaving 1 mm of wire above the vise jaws. Tap the end of the wire with the ball-peen hammer until a nail head forms. Remove the wire and trim it to a ½" (1.2 cm) nail. Repeat this step three times [figure 10].

10 To assemble, start from the back with the copper sheet. Stack the layers onto the nails, placing crimp tubes between each layer. Place tape over the back of the copper sheet to keep the nails in place while riveting [figure 11].

11 Place the brooch, frame side up, on the flat anvil. Trim the nails to about 1–1.5 mm above the frame and carefully tap flush with a ball-peen hammer. Repeat on all corners [figure 12].

Copper Patina

Put the clean copper sheet in a covered plastic container. Pour a small amount of straight ammonia over the sheet, leaving a small puddle of ammonia in the container—but not covering the piece. Sprinkle a small amount of table salt over the piece, put the lid on the container, and let it sit overnight. The next day, rinse the sheet and let it air-dry. Because the patina can have a flaky or chalky texture, coat it with several layers of clear matte acrylic spray.

For another patina effect, try liver of sulfur to blacken the copper, then use a Pro-Polish pad to remove the excess oxidation.

ALSO USED IN:

Trio Bangles with Recycled Tin Charms

DESIGNED BY:
Beth Taylor

FINISHED SIZE:
2¾" diameter (6.9 cm)

WHEN I FIRST STARTED USING FOUND OBJECTS
and recycled materials in my jewelry, tin cans quickly became
a favorite material. But because heat will ruin the tin, cold
connections also became integral to my jewelry pieces.
This fun bracelet celebrates both the use of cold connections
and the tin can—not to mention my love of charm bracelets!

materials

22-gauge sterling silver sheet

Metal from assorted tin cans: cookie tins, tea tins, coffee cans, etc.

2½' (76.2 cm) of sterling silver 14-gauge round wire

15 sterling silver 16- or 18-gauge 10.8mm closed jump rings

15 sterling silver 18-gauge 7.5mm jump rings

15 miniature brass nails, ⅜" long x .020" diameter

2 miniature #0-80, ⅜" long fillister-head brass bolts

2 sterling silver 3x3mm crimp tubes

tools

Flush cutters

Ruler

Fine-tip permanent marker

Chasing hammer

Steel bench block or anvil

Center punch (slim automatic or regular)

Flex shaft, drill, or Dremel tool

Drill bits: #52, #55, and #75

Flat/half-round pliers

Riveting hammer

Bench pin or clamped wooden block

Round bracelet mandrel

Rawhide or plastic mallet

Soft scrub brush

Dishwashing liquid

Rubber gloves

Liver of sulfur or Midas Black Max

Pro-Polish polishing pads

Rotary tumbler and steel shot [optional]

1 sheet full-page label paper

Scissors

Jeweler's saw frame

#2/0 saw blades

Joyce Chen kitchen scissors

Goo Gone

Half-round or flat, triangle, or square needle files

High-speed cylinder burr (6+ mm)

400- and 600-grit wet/dry sandpaper for metal

Windex

Wax paper

Clear Krylon acrylic non-yellowing spray-on sealer

Miniature chamois or muslin buff [optional]

ZAM polish [optional]

Miniature screwdriver

2 pairs of chain-nose pliers

Disc cutter: 8mm disc size

Ring clamp

Household flat-head hammer

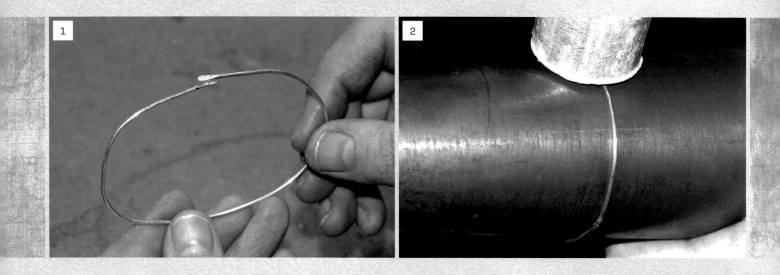

note

The length will be about ³/₈" (9.5 mm) longer than the actual finished size to account for design overlap and hammering.

1   Choose your bracelet size using the chart below and use flush cutters to cut 3 lengths of 14-gauge wire.

SIZE	INNER DIAMETER	APPROXIMATE FINAL CIRCUMFERENCE	LENGTH OF WIRE NEEDED
Small	2¼" (5.7 cm)	7" (17.7 cm)	7³/₈" (18.7 cm)
Medium	2½" (6.3 cm)	7⁷/₈" (20 cm)	8¼" (20.9 cm)
Large	2¾" (6.9 cm)	8⁵/₈" (21.9 cm)	9" (22.8 cm)
X-Large	3" (7.6 cm)	9½" (24.1 cm)	9⁷/₈" (25 cm)

2   Measure and mark ¼" (6.3 mm) in from both ends of all 3 wires with the permanent marker.

3   Using the flat end of a chasing hammer, flatten each end of the wire from the tip to the mark, then file to round the ends of all 3 wires.

4   Lay the wire horizontally on your work surface. Measure 2 mm from the right end of one wire and make a dot with the marker. Measure 2 mm from that dot and make another dot mark. Measure 4 mm in from the left end of the wire and make a dot.

5   Center punch and drill all 3 marks with a #75 drill bit.

6   Use flat/half-round pliers to bend the wire into an oval shape, keeping the flat ends parallel to your work surface ensuring drilled holes will meet facing up. Overlap with 2 drilled holes on top. Insert a miniature nail through the top of the wire and through 2 end holes [figure 1].

7   Invert the bangle and rest it on the steel bench block or anvil with the shaft of the nail pointing straight up. Snip the nail shaft with flush cutters, leaving about 2–3 mm remaining. Rivet the nail in place.

8   Turn the bangle right-side up. Position the bangle so it rests securely over the corner of a bench-pin or clamped wooden block. Use a #75 drill bit and the second hole as your guide to drill through both bangle wires. Insert the miniature nail and rivet.

9   Repeat Steps 4–8 with the remaining 2 bangles.

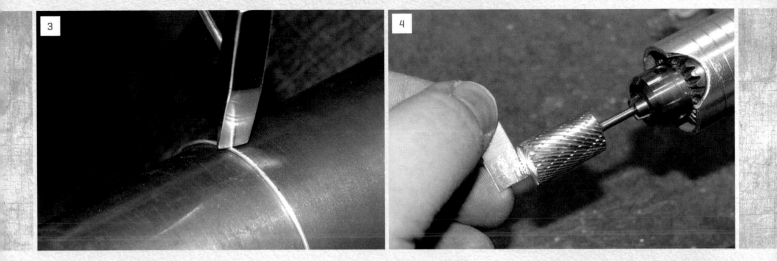

10 Slide 1 bangle over your round bracelet mandrel, pushing it down as far as it will go. Tap the bangle with the rawhide or plastic mallet to shape into a uniform circle. Remove bangle from mandrel and place on a flat surface. If the bangle does not lie evenly on the surface, place the bangle on the steel bench block or anvil and tap gently with your mallet until even. Repeat with remaining 2 bangles [figure 2].

11 Place the bangles back on the bracelet mandrel, one at a time, and use the chisel-shaped end of the riveting hammer to tap the bracelet and make hammer marks all the way around [figure 3]. This process may have slightly altered the shape of your bangles. Remove the bangle from the mandrel and use a rawhide mallet to flatten. Set bangles aside.

12 Texture both sides of all the sterling silver closed jump rings, one at a time, on the bench block or anvil using the chisel-end of the riveting hammer. Open all the 4.5mm jump rings and slide 1 closed ring onto each. Close all the small jump rings.

13 Wash the bangles with a soft scrub brush and a drop of dishwashing liquid. Wear rubber gloves to prevent transfer of skin oils to the metal. Rinse and dry. Darken with either liver of sulfur or Midas Black Max. Wash again and dry. Polish with a Pro-Polish pad until you achieve the desired patina. *Optional: Tumble polish the bangles and rings for about 20 minutes in a rotary tumbler with mixed steel shot, water, and drop of dishwashing liquid. After tumbling, remove, dry, and set aside.*

14 Draw an 8 x 17 mm rectangle on label paper. Cut out the rectangle and affix it to the 22-gauge sterling silver sheet. Use a jeweler's saw frame and #2/0 saw blade to saw out the rectangle.

15 On label paper, draw a smaller 6 x 15 mm rectangle. Cut out the rectangle and affix to the tin. Cut the rectangle out of tin using Joyce Chen kitchen scissors. Remove the stickers from the silver and tin. If the label paper is hard to remove, you can use a product like Goo Gone to remove it. Do a spot-check on your tin first to make sure the product won't damage the tin. File the edges of the silver and tin rectangles, slightly rounding the corners.

16 Insert the cylinder burr into the flex shaft and run the burr over the silver rectangle to add texture to the metal [figure 4].

TIP

Stick the label paper on the inside of the tin, where there is no coloring, to avoid possible damage to the surface of the tin.

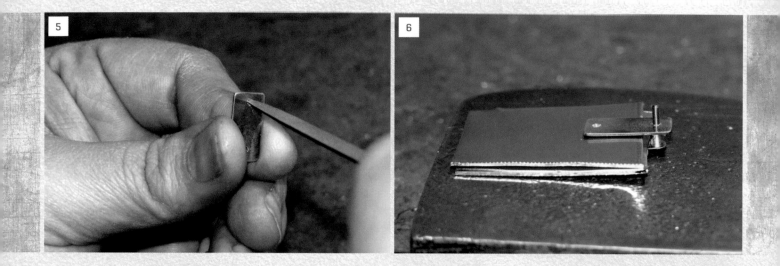

17 Sand both sides of the silver rectangle and the edges of the tin rectangle, first with 400-grit sandpaper and then with 600-grit sandpaper.

18 Use the fine-tip marker to make a dot at the top middle of the tin rectangle, about 2 mm from the edge. Repeat at the other end. Center punch and drill with a #52 drill bit. Wipe the tin rectangle clean with Windex. Place the piece on wax paper and seal with the clear acrylic spray-on sealer to prevent rusting. Let dry and repeat on reverse side.

19 Center the tin rectangle on top of silver rectangle. Holding both in place, use the holes in the tin rectangle as a template to mark holes on the silver rectangle beneath. Remove the tin rectangle. Center punch and drill the silver rectangle with a #55 drill bit. Insert and turn the tip of the triangle needle file to slightly enlarge the holes [figure 5].

20 Patina the silver rectangle using liver of sulfur or the Midas Black Max. Wash and dry. Use a Pro-Polish pad to remove the excess patina. If you prefer a higher shine, lightly polish the silver using a flex shaft, buff, and a bit of ZAM polish.

21 Insert 1 brass #0-80 fillister-head bolt through the top hole in the tin rectangle. Thread a 3x3mm sterling silver crimp tube onto the shaft of the bolt, then insert it into the top hole on the silver rectangle. The bolt will be tight. Using your miniature screwdriver, turn the bolt until it is all the way through the silver rectangle.

22 Lay the tin and silver rectangle piece tin-side down on your bench block or anvil, with the bolt shaft pointing straight up in the air. Insert several pieces of scrap metal between the pieces of silver and tin until the silver is fully supported and horizontal. Snip off the shaft of the bolt, leaving a tiny amount of the bolt exposed above the silver. Rivet the end to form a tight join [figure 6].

23 Remove the pieces of scrap metal. Slide the 3 bangles between the tin and silver layers. Insert the other brass #0-80 fillister-head bolt into the second hole and thread on the remaining 3x3mm crimp tube, swiveling the tin if needed. Screw the bolt through the silver rectangle using the miniature screwdriver. Snip off the shaft leaving a tiny amount of the bolt exposed and rivet to form a tight join. The 3 bangles should now be securely connected and able to slide freely through the connector [figure 7].

24 Cut 30 circles of tin with an 8mm disc cutter, making 15 double-sided charms. Center punch the middle of the top of one circle. Place another circle back to back with the first circle and grasp together with the ring clamp. Drill through both layers using a #75 drill bit. Insert a miniature nail through the hole, snip off the shaft, and rivet until flush. Repeat for a total of 15 charms.

25 Center punch about 2 mm from the top of the circle charm. Grasp with the ring clamp and drill with a #55 drill bit [figure 8].

26 File and sand with 400-grit sandpaper to smooth the edges. Clean the charms with Windex. Place the charms on wax paper and spray with clear acrylic spray-on sealer. When dry, turn over and repeat. Let dry completely.

27 Open one of the jump rings attached to the sterling silver closed ring charm. Add a tin circle charm and attach the jump ring to one of the bangles; close the jump ring. Repeat with remaining charms, attaching 5 charms to each bangle.

Polymer Clay Pendant

DESIGNED BY:
Robert Dancik

FINISHED SIZE:
**3¹/₂" high x 1³/₄" wide
(8.9 cm x 4.45 cm)**

WE ARE CONSTANTLY MOVING THROUGH TIME AND SPACE simultaneously. We cannot separate these movements, for even at rest, we are moving. I wondered what an instrument that measures both concurrently might look like. Would it be a clock or a compass? What if the two were combined? This piece is a prototype for me of just such an instrument.

materials

Premo polymer clay: ¹/₈ block each of ecru, translucent, and black

3" x 3" (7.6 x 7.6 cm) of copper 22-gauge sheet

6" (15.2 cm) of copper 16-gauge wire, cut in half

4 #2-56 Phillips-head ³/₄" (1.9 cm) bolts with nuts

1 #0-80 bolt and nut

1 pearl, bead, or other adornment

tools

White paper

2 wooden ¹/₈" (3.1 mm) dowels or similar

Polymer clay rolling pin

Needle tool or similar

Circle template or similar

Toaster oven (designated for non-food use)

Ruler

Fine-tip permanent marker

Jeweler's saw frame

#2/0 saw blades

Bench pin

Texturing tools

Ball-peen hammer

Bench block or similar

Liver of sulfur

Center punch

Drill or flex shaft

Drill bits: #52 and #48

Round-nose pliers

Flat-nose pliers

Half round file, #2 cut

Silicone carbide (wet/dry) 400- and 600-grit sandpaper

Scribe or similar

Burnt umber acrylic paint

Soft cloth

Craft knife

Brown wax shoe polish

Alcohol inks and applicator or Q-tip

Diagonal wire cutters

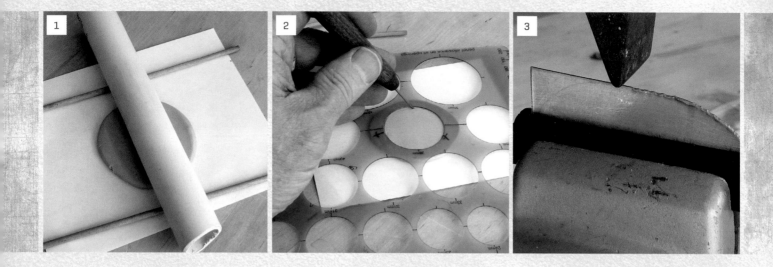

1   Condition together ⅛ blocks each of ecru and translucent polymer clay. Condition the black clay. To condition the clay, roll it into a ball with your hands, then twist the clay and roll it into a ball again. Continue working the clay until it is soft and malleable.

2   On a piece of clean white paper, place two ⅛" (3.1 mm) dowels parallel to each other and place half of the conditioned ecru/translucent clay between the dowels. Place the rolling pin on the dowels and roll the clay out [figure 1].

3   Using a needle tool and circle template as a guide, cut out a disc that is 1⅜" (3.4 cm) in diameter from the rolled-out clay [figure 2]. Rub some of the conditioned black polymer clay onto the top of each Phillips-head bolt, filling the grooves. Bake the clay disc and bolts according to the clay manufacturer's directions in the toaster oven and allow them to cool.

4   While the clay is baking, draw a 1¾" x 2⅜" (4.4 x 6 cm) rectangle on the 22-gauge copper sheet. Using the circle template, draw a 1¾" (4.4 cm) semicircle at one end of the copper; this will be the top of the piece. If you want to texture the copper, do so now, before you saw out the shape. Saw, file, and sand the copper smooth.

5   Texture the edges of the copper. Patina the copper with liver of sulfur [figure 3].

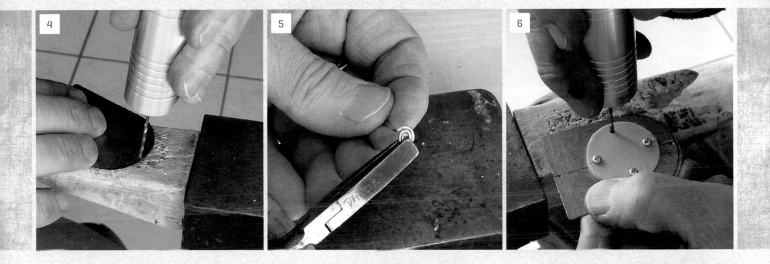

6   Center punch and drill 2 holes, centered and ⅛" [3.1 mm] in from the top and bottom edges, in the copper with a #52 drill bit [figure 4].

7   Flatten 1" [2.5 cm] of one of the pieces of copper wire with the flat face of the hammer and make a spiral at the flattened end. With the flat-nose pliers, make a 90 degree bend where the spiral meets the shaft of the wire [figure 5].

8   With the other wire, flatten the entire length with the flat face of the hammer and file the end of this wire to a shallow point. Patina both wires as you did the copper sheet.

9   Using the circle template, mark the 4 cardinal directions (north, south, east, west) on the polymer clay disc and drill a #48 drill-bit hole in from the edge at each point. File the edges of the disc to round them a bit. Using lots of water, sand the disc with 400-grit then 600-grit wet/dry sandpaper.

10   Position the disc on the copper sheet about ⅜" [9.5 mm] down from the top and with the holes oriented to the top, bottom, right, and left of the piece. "Key" the disc by making a mark on both the disc and the copper so you know the orientation of the two.

11   Using the polymer clay disc as a guide, use a #52 drill bit to drill 1 hole in the copper and insert a bolt into the hole to keep the disc in position. Drill another hole and insert another bolt. Drill the next 2 holes. Remove the polymer disc [figure 6].

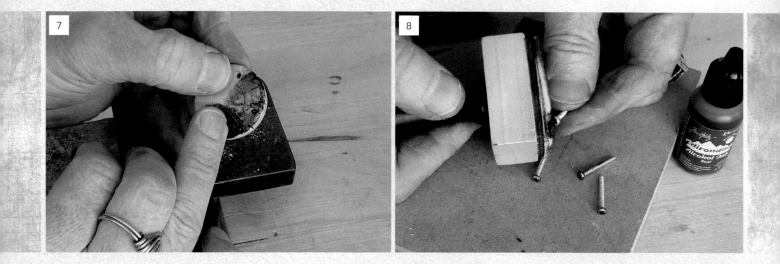

12 Inscribe the disc as desired (I had a compass in mind for my piece). Rub the acrylic paint
on the surface of the disc and rub off the excess, leaving the paint on the inscribed lines
[figure 7]. Sand again with the 600-grit sandpaper, then turn the paper over on the
paper side and rub vigorously (I know this sounds odd—but it really works). Rub the piece
in your hand and then with a soft cloth; this deposits a bit of oil on the piece and the
rubbing brings up a soft sheen. To make the faint "craze" lines, run a sharp craft knife
over the polymer clay a few times in random directions. Rub a very little bit of brown
shoe polish on the piece; let it dry for an hour or more. Rub with a soft cloth to bring up
a soft polished surface. Alternately, you can buff the piece with an unsewn plain muslin
buff on a polishing machine.

13 Sand and polish the polymer clay inlays in the screws, as you did the disc above, to
expose the black cross in each bolt head. Using the alcohol inks on an applicator or Q-tip,
color the metal part on the head of each bolt and allow them to dry **[figure 8]**.

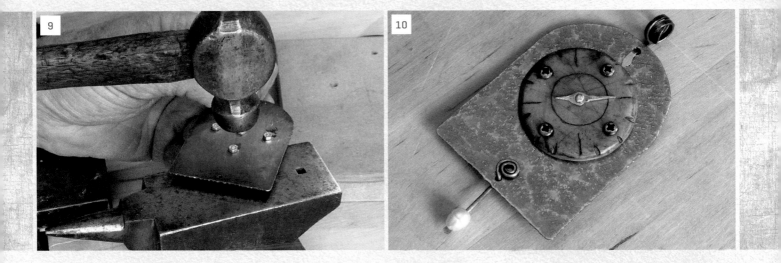

14 Attach the polymer clay disc with the Phillips-head bolts and nuts. Tighten the nuts with pliers. Turn the piece over so that 1 bolt head sits on the metal bench block. Trim each bolt down to the nut with a diagonal cutter, leaving just a tiny bit of the shaft to rivet. Use the ball-peen hammer to rivet the bit of exposed bolt down against the nut, locking it into position [figure 9].

15 Cut, file, sand, and patina a copper appliqué for the center of the piece (I cut a pointer for my compass). Center punch and drill a #52 drill-bit hole in the center of the appliqué and position it on top of the disc. Using the appliqué as a guide, drill through the polymer clay and the copper and attach the appliqué with a #0-80 nut and bolt. Finish as the bolts above.

16 Insert the pointed wire through the hole at the top of the copper from front to back. Bend the wire up in the back of the piece and the point down so that it lies flat against the front of the copper. Using round-nose pliers, roll the wire down until it almost reaches the top of the copper to form a bail. Insert the spiraled wire, front to back, through the hole at the bottom of the piece and bend the wire down in the back and the spiral up in the front of the piece so that the spiral lies flat against the front of the copper sheet. Add the pearl or other bead. Cut to the desired length and hammer the end of the wire to stop the bead from sliding off [figure 10].

Found Object Sandwich Ring

DESIGNED BY:
Thomas Mann

FINISHED SIZE:
2¼" high x 1½" wide
(5.72 cm x 3.81 cm)

DESIGNING A RING THAT CAN CHANGE SIZES EASILY
has always been a design goal. With this project I had the
opportunity to blend several design intentions together. This ring
is sizable from a size 6 to a size 10. Just loosen the shank screw
with an eyeglass screwdriver and slide to adjust and tighten.

materials

Frame and ring shank templates

Bronze or brass 22-gauge sheet: 3" x 3" (7.6 x 7.6 cm)

Nickel or sterling silver 20-gauge sheet: 4½" x 3" (11.4 x 7.6 cm)

Patterned bronze or brass 24-gauge sheet (or plain): 3" x 3" (7.6 x 7.6 cm)

¹⁄₁₆" (1.5 mm) clear 3" x 3" (7.6 x 7.6 cm) acrylic sheet

1" (2.5 cm) of brass or copper 18-gauge wire

5" (12.7 cm) of sterling silver or copper 16-gauge wire

Collage elements (your choice) or shown: green Plexiglas disc, bird stud, clear drilled Plexiglas disc, rose flower, numeral 4, plastic star, and threaded metal ball

Photo to fit in 1¼" x ⁷⁄₈" (3.1 x 2.2 cm) window but extends beyond edges of the façade layer.

6 brass #0-80 hex-head machine screws (bolts)

3 stainless steel #0-80 slotted pan-head screws

5 brass #0-80 hex nuts

4 stainless steel #0 washers

2 stainless steel #2 washers

tools

Photocopier

Scissors

Rubber cement

Center punch

Flex shaft, Dremel tool, or drill press*

Drill bits: #52, #55, and #60

Steel bench block

Jeweler's saw frame

#2/0 saw blades

Chasing tools or decorative punch

Riveting hammer

Planishing hammer (optional)

Snap-On sanding disc and mandrel bit

Metal files various sizes and cuts or 4–6" half-round/flat file

Fine-tip permanent marker

Scribe

0-80 tap (threader) in a pin-vise handle

Flap wheel bit, or 220-grit sandpaper

Steel wool (medium)

Ring mandrel

Rawhide, fiber or nylon mallet

Half round/flat combo-nose pliers

Oxidation agent (liver of sulfur, JAX silver blackener)

Brass brush

Round-nose pliers

Chain-nose pliers

Flush cutters (side cutter)

Ruler

Canned air

0-80 bolt and nut driver (miniature socket driver)

Small ball-peen hammer

Cyanoacrylate (super) glue

Finishing drum bit or cylindrical abrasive rubber bit

chuck must accommodate very small drill diameters

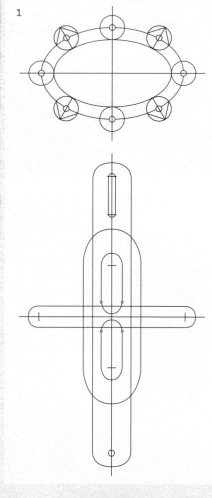

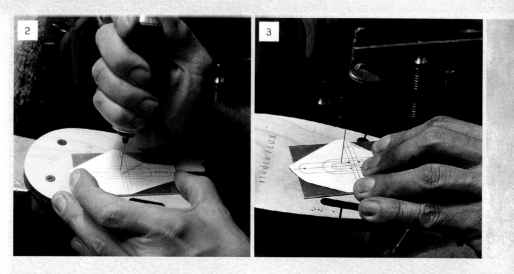

1 Photocopy the templates (copy paper adheres the best) and broadly scissor out the patterns. Using rubber cement, adhere the frame façade template to the bronze or brass 22-gauge sheet and the ring shank template to the nickel 20-gauge sheet **[figure 1]**.

2 Center punch and drill all the marked holes in the frame with a #55 drill bit.

3 Ring shank: Drill out the 4 "center" holes in the ring shank with a #60 drill bit or smaller **[figure 2]**. Drill out the 4 holes that make up the "T" shape in the shank with a #52 drill bit. Drill out the sizing hole in the shank with a #55 drill bit. Drill a hole (any of the bit sizes) in the interior of the slot shape.

4 Using the jeweler's saw frame and #2/0 saw blade, pierce (saw) out the U-shaped lines that connect the holes in the T shape in the ring shank and pierce (saw) out the interior slot **[figure 3]**.

5 Drill a hole in the interior of the façade frame and pierce (saw) out the oval shape.

6 Saw out the exterior design of the façade frame and ring shank and remove the paper patterns.

note

All chasing and center punching must be done on a hardened steel bench block.

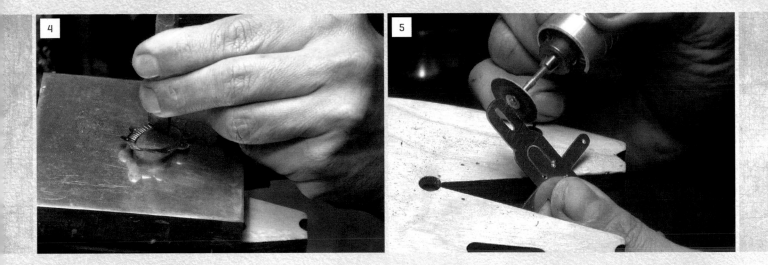

note

If you chase the façade frame as intensely as depicted here, you'll have to correct the distortion to the frame that the chasing action will make.

7 Use a chasing tool to texture the façade frame and hallmark the ring shank (if you don't have a hallmarking stamp, you can use letter stamps). Flip it over on the bench block and tap it flat with the flat face of the rivet hammer (in the illustration, I am using a planishing hammer). You might also add a textured design using an electro etching tool or by employing an acid-etching technique **[figure 4]**.

8 File the interior edge and flat surfaces of the façade frame with a Snap-On sanding disc or hand file.

9 File the ring shank with a Snap-On sanding disc bit or hand file and set aside **[figure 5]**.

10 Place the façade frame over your photo, aligning it as you deem appropriate. Use the façade frame as a template for drilling #55 holes in the photo layer. Once you decide where you want it, drill through the frame and photo with a #55 drill bit, holding the pieces tight so the alignment is correct. (You can also mark the holes through the frame with a fine-tip permanent marker, remove the frame, and drill out the marked holes in the photo with a #55 drill bit.) Mark the "top" of the frame with the fine-tip permanent marker or scribe so you know the proper alignment.

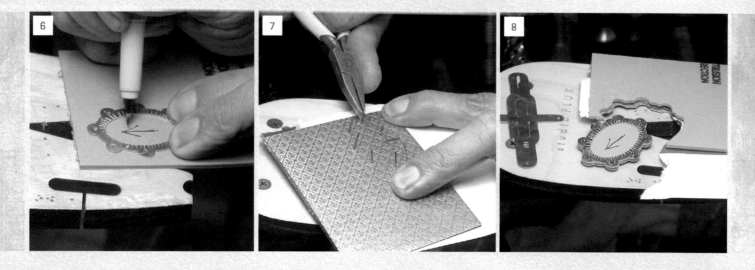

note

The assembly of all of the layers of the
"sandwich" depends on all of these holes
being drilled accurately .

11 Place the façade frame over the ¹/₁₆" (1.5 mm) acrylic sheet, hold tightly together, and
either drill holes through the frame and acrylic with a #55 drill bit or use the permanent
marker to mark the holes in the acrylic, remove the frame, and drill the acrylic with a #55
drill bit. Mark the "top" and front of the acrylic with the permanent marker **[figure 6]**.

12 Place the façade frame over the back side of the patterned metal, hold tightly, and drill
through the frame and patterned metal with a #55 drill bit (or use the permanent marker
to mark the holes through the frame onto the metal, remove the frame, and drill out the
holes in the metal).

13 In the following order, sandwich the frame, clear acrylic, photo, and patterned metal
back using sterling silver or copper 16-gauge wire rivets as placeholders for the final
rivets. Use just 2 rivets at first on the top and bottom to get the proper alignment, then
add the rest of the rivets. Bend the rivets toward the center of the sandwich and push
them down as tightly as possible in order to tighten the layers together **[figure 7]**.

14 Using the façade frame layer as a template, and sawing along its edge, saw through the
other 3 layers to create the ring top shape from the sandwich **[figure 8]**.

15 File the edge of the ring top shape first from the back to the front, then front to the back,
to level all of the layers together with the façade frame layer. Finally, use the steel wool
to smooth and refine and finish the edge of the piece.

16 Unbend the rivets and take the sandwich layers apart. Mark the back side of the frame
with the permanent marker or scribe on the "top" of the acrylic, if you haven't done so
already.

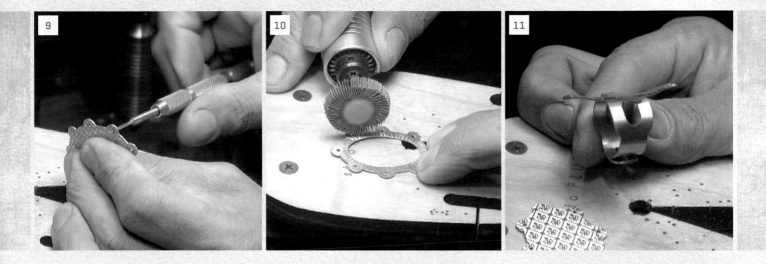

17 The holes that accommodated the rivets are smaller than the holes that will accommodate the bolts. So, the holes in the front 3 layers, the façade frame, the acrylic and photograph layers must be drilled out with a #52 drill creating a "pass hole." Do not drill out the back layer as this layer will be tapped (threaded), and the #55 hole that is already there is just the right size for tapping.

18 Tap (thread) the remaining 4 holes with the 0-80 tap through the back of the rear layer (which is also the patterned or plain surface layer) [figure 9].

19 Tap (thread) the sizing hole in the ring shank with the 0-80 tap.

20 Use a sand disc or file on the back edge of the façade frame and the edge of the rear layer to remove the raised burr edge.

21 Flap wheel, or sand disc, or just steel wool the front of the façade frame and both sides of the ring shank [figure 10].

22 Bend the ring shank with your hands around a ring mandrel; the T-shape wings will emerge during this process. Use a nylon or rawhide (soft faced) mallet to shape the band close to the approximate size.

23 Use half-round flat-nose combo pliers to bend and shape the T-shaped arms upward, so the holes line up to the faced frame holes [figure 11].

24 Use the #52 drill bit to drill holes in the collage elements (rose, plastic star, numeral 4).

25 Patina the frame, the patterned metal back, ring shank, and collage elements with liver of sulfur or JAX silver blackener. Rub with steel wool and a brass brush to finish; set aside.

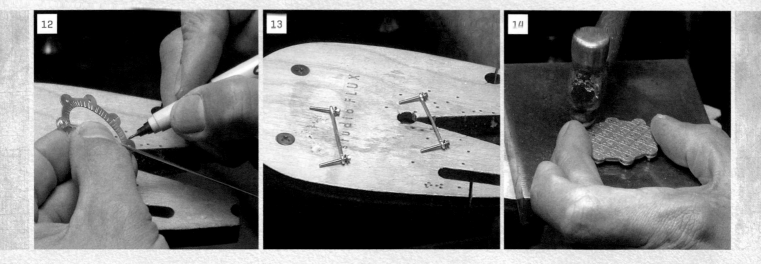

26 Use round-nose pliers to make a loop on one end of a piece of sterling silver 16-gauge wire; position over the holes in the frame to mark where the second loop should be. The wires will be attached top left hole to bottom right hole and top right hole to bottom left hole. Nip the wire and make the opposite loop. Bend with pliers to make them even. [You can also measure the distance between the holes and mark with a permanent marker on a piece of sterling silver 16-gauge wire and make the loops that way.] Repeat for the second wire [figure 12].

27 Put a #0 stainless steel washer onto 4 brass #0-80 hex-head machine screws and put through the wire collage elements; set aside [figure 13].

28 Line up your sandwich pieces. Take the paper off the acrylic layer [back side first] and hold onto the sides to avoid fingerprints. Immediately mate with the photo layer. Then add the façade frame and rear layers. Hold the sandwich elements together. Use canned air to get the dust out between the acrylic and photo layers, if necessary.

29 Using a 0-80 nut driver and the hex-head screws from Step 27, attach the wire elements to the threaded holes of the sandwich frame, one at a time. Nip each screw from behind leaving 1–1.5 mm and set with the ball-peen end of the small rivet hammer [figure 14].

30 At this point in the process, you could be making your own decisions about what elements to add to your compositions. What follows is a description of the elements I decided to add and how they were attached. Feel free to be creative!

Drill a hole in the green disc with a #60 drill bit. Use the disc as a template for placing it over the acrylic layer covering the photo. Drill through the acrylic, photo, and rear layer with a #60 drill bit. Use a brass or copper 18-gauge wire rivet to attach. Nip and set with a ball-peen hammer.

31 Insert the bird stud through the clear drilled Plexiglas disc and thread a #0-80 brass hex nut all the way onto the screw against the back of the disc to hold the disc in place and act as a spacer. Insert that assembly through the top #52 drilled hole of the ring shank. Thread on a #0-80 brass hex nut on the back side [ring armature side] and tighten to snug but do not tighten all the way. You want to leave some wiggle room for the other bolts to find their way through the remaining holes.

note

Be gentle; you are not setting the bolt as you would a rivet. You are just expanding the bolt shaft slightly so that it won't back out of the threaded hole. You want to round it over and make it pretty!

note

I made the bird stud by silver soldering a #0-80 hex-head machine screw to the back of the bird charm. If you have a torch and the know-how, you can make an easily attachable studded ornament out of any metal object that can be soldered.

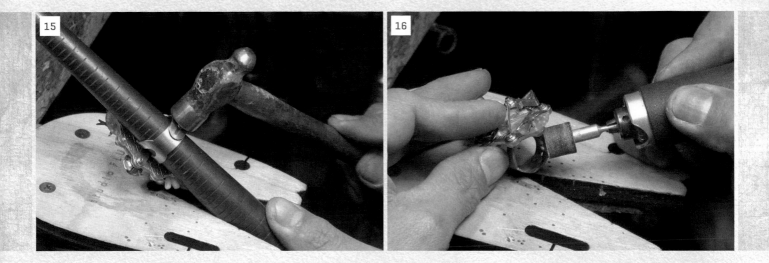

32 To attach the star, thread a #0-80 hex head screw from the ring armature side into the bottom threaded hole of the photo package and up through all of the layers, the star, and one #2 stainless washer. Twist on the drilled and threaded brass ball and tighten gently. A little bit of cyanoacrylate (super) glue inside the ball will assure its connection to the threads.

33 Tighten the top ring (armature side) nut.

34 Put a #0-80 stainless steel slotted pan-head screw into the numeral "4" element with a #2 stainless washer behind the "4" and attach through the package and ring shank with a #0-80 brass hex nut.

35 Put a #0-80 stainless steel slotted pan-head screw through the rose flower element, then through the package and ring shank and attach it with a #0-80 brass hex nut.

36 Set the back side of the bird, disc, and brass hex nut over leather with a ball-peen hammer, being careful to not damage the plastic elements.

37 Set the "4" hex nut with a ball-peen hammer. Again, you are not setting them like a rivet, you just want to prevent the bolt from backing out.

38 Thread a stainless steel #0-80 pan-head slotted screw into the "sizing" hole in the shank and nip off the bolt stem inside the shank with flush-cutting pliers. Once the proper size is determined, you can tighten the screw all the way. To "set" the screw, slide the ring so it is tight onto the ring mandrel. Use the small riveting hammer's flat face to set the screw by hammering the head of the screw against the mandrel. If you ever want to change the ring size, simply turn the screw out, resize the ring, insert a new screw and reset as above. You can remove any remaining abrasion points from the set screw on the interior of the band with a half-round file, a drum mandrel bit (pictured), a cylindrical abrasive rubber bit, or simply with a finger of steel wool—or a combination of all of these tools [figures 15 and 16]. Voilà! A Found Object Sandwich Ring!

Bowl of Gems Earrings

DESIGNED BY:
Kate Richbourg

FINISHED SIZE:
2 ⁵⁄₈" long x ½" wide
(6.7 cm x 1.27 cm)

WHEN I DESIGN, I START BY MAKING LITTLE PILES OF BEADS to look at how they work with each other. I literally took a small cluster of beads that I had piled on my work table and placed them in a dapped disc. I loved the way that they looked like a little bowlful of gems. Adding them to a swingy earring design just made them more appealing to me!

materials

4" (10.1 cm) of copper 14-gauge wire

9" (22.8 cm) of sterling silver 20-gauge round wire

24" (60.9 cm) of sterling silver 28-gauge round wire

2 sterling silver 24-gauge ½" (1.2cm) round discs

2 copper 24-gauge ½" (1.2cm) round discs

2 sterling silver 18-gauge 3.5mm ID jump rings

20 size 2–3mm beads: crystals, pearls, and seed beads

1 pair of sterling silver ear wires

tools

Flush cutters

Fine tip permanent marker

Riveting hammer

Steel bench block

Dot and asterisk design stamps

Ball-peen hammer

1.8 mm hole-punch pliers

1.25 mm hole-punch pliers

Dapping block and punches

Table vise

Chain-nose pliers

Liver of sulfur

Pro-Polish polishing pad

Round-nose pliers

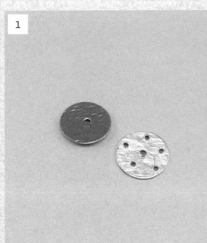

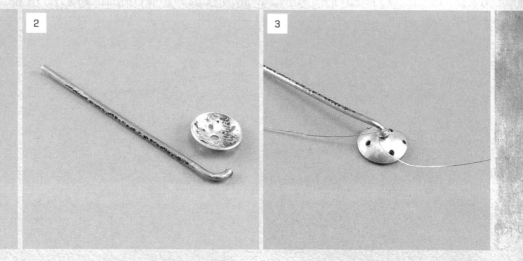

1   Cut the copper 14-gauge wire in half. Use the permanent marker to mark a line ¼"
(6.3 mm) from each end on the wires. Texture the middle 1½" (3.8 cm) of the wires using
the chisel end of the riveting hammer, leaving the ¼" (6.3 mm) on each end smooth.

2   Texture one side of each sterling silver disc with the riveting hammer only. Turn the discs
over and texture the other side using the riveting hammer and the dot and asterisk design
stamps. Texture one side of each copper disc with the chisel end of the riveting hammer.
Gently texture the jump rings the same way.

3   Use the 1.8 mm hole-punch pliers to punch a hole in the center of all of the discs. Use the
1.25 mm hole-punch pliers to randomly punch 5–6 more holes in each silver disc [figure 1].

4   Place 1 silver disc with the asterisk- and dot-stamped side up in the corresponding-sized
indentation in the dapping block. Gently dome the disc. The stamping may smooth out a
bit, but it will still be visible. Repeat with the other silver disc.

5   Insert one of the copper wires between the jaws of the table vise. Leave about 2mm of wire
sticking above the jaws and use the riveting hammer to make a nail head on the end of
the wire. Remove the wire from the vise. Using chain-nose pliers, grasp the wire about ⅛"
(3.1 mm) from the nail head and bend the wire to a right angle. Repeat this step with the
other copper wire.

6   Patina the wire and discs with liver of sulfur and polish with a Pro-Polish pad [figure 2].

7   Slide each of the copper wires through the center hole in the silver discs so the wire sticks
straight up against the back of the dome.

8   Cut 12" (30.4 cm) of 28-gauge sterling silver wire. Position the middle of the sterling wire
on the back of one of the silver discs, on the copper wire. Wrap the silver wire around the
copper wire so that the disc pushes tightly against the nail head [figure 3].

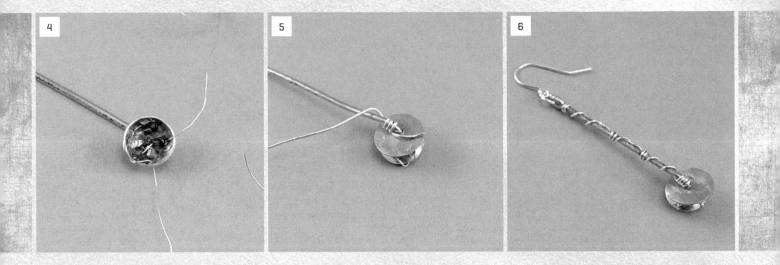

9   Thread each end of the silver wire through different holes in the front of the disc. Add 1–3 beads onto each wire, then thread the wire back through the disc and up through a different hole. Alternating between each end of the wire, add beads to create a free-form weave in the "cup" **[figure 4]**. When you have finished wrapping, hide the ends of the silver wire among the wraps and trim the excess.

10 Repeat Steps 0 and 9 with the other copper wire and silver disc.

11 Slide 1 copper disc onto each copper wire, with the textured side facing the dome of the silver disc. Attach an ear wire to each jump ring. Using round-nose pliers, make a simple loop at the top of each copper wire. Attach a jump ring to each simple loop.

12 Using 4½" [11.4 cm] of 20-gauge sterling wire, wrap the wire four times around one of the copper wires, behind the copper disc **[figure 5]**. Proceed to wrap the remaining wire up the copper wire, creating decorative bends in the wire with your pliers as you wrap. Finish with 2 or 3 wraps below the top loop **[figure 6]**. Trim the excess wire and press the end against the copper wire with chain-nose pliers. Repeat with the other earring.

Honing Owl Pendant

DESIGNED BY:
Lisa and Scott Cylinder

FINISHED SIZE:
2½" wide x 3¼" high
(6.35 cm x 8.25 cm)

SCOTT AND I BOTH ENJOY THE OBSERVATION OF NATURE and draw our narratives from these experiences. Our sources and inspirations are two-fold. They are a combination of observations of nature and man-made objects of special beauty or intrigue. The result is our "man-made" object, which incorporates other man-made object(s) whose references and imagery are derived from nature.

materials

Found object (shown: vintage Kenberry scissor sharpener)

3" x 4" (7.6 x 10.1 cm) of copper 22-gauge sheet (body)

½" x 1" (1.2 x 2.5 cm) of sterling silver 22-gauge sheet (tail)

3" x 3" (7.6 x 7.6 cm) of sterling silver 24-gauge sheet (feathers)

6" (15.2 cm) of copper ³/₃₂" (2.3 mm) diameter tubing

tools

Fine-tip permanent marker

Jeweler's saw frame

#1/0 saw blade

Center punch

Drill bit gauge

Flex shaft or drill press

#42 drill bit

Half-round/flat file, #2 cut

Sandpaper: 400- and 600-grit

Chasing hammer

Texturing tools

Anvil

Rawhide mallet

Ruler

Dapping tools

Vise

Ball-peen hammer or riveting hammer

Chain-nose pliers

Brass or satin brush

Liver of sulfur or Midas Black Max

#0000 steel wool

Prong pusher or burnishing tool

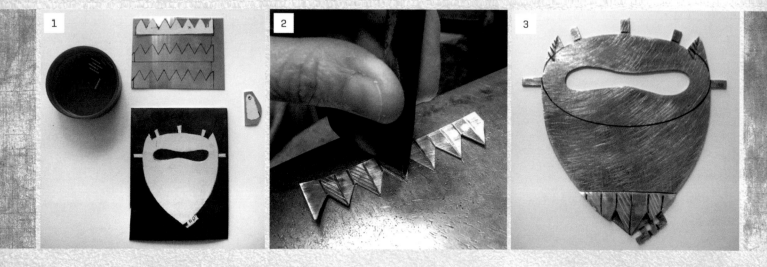

1 Trace the outline of the body and eye design on copper 22-gauge sheet. Trace the tail design on sterling silver 22-gauge sheet. Trace 3 rows of feathers on sterling silver 24-gauge sheet.

2 Using the jeweler's saw frame and #1/0 saw blade, cut out the body, tail piece, and 3 rows of feathers [figure 1].

3 Center punch and use the #42 drill bit to drill a hole in the eye shape and the feet shape. Saw out the pieces.

4 File and sand all surfaces.

5 Texture the ears and feet of the body and the tail and feather strips using a chasing hammer and texturing tools on an anvil. Flatten the metal with a rawhide mallet [figure 2].

6 Mark the body piece where you plan to attach your found object(s).

7 Place a row of feathers starting at the bottom of the body. Trace the body shape onto the feather row, then use the jeweler's saw frame and #1/0 saw blade to remove the excess feather metal. You will have enough feather material for 6 rows of feathers [figure 3].

feathers

tail

body and eyes

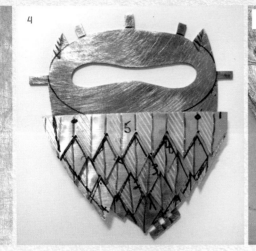

4

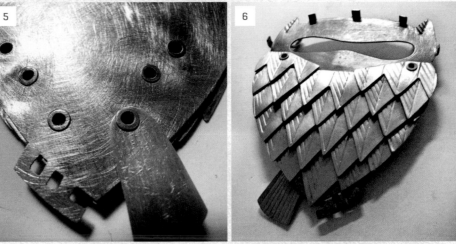

5 6

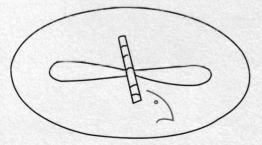

beak on found object

note

Use the drill bit gauge or make a test hole in some scrap metal to check your bit size. You want to make sure it's a tight fit for the tubing.

8 Repeat for all the feather rows, marking the tube rivet placement on each piece with a permanent marker. There are 2 rivets per row. Be aware of your rivet locations and make sure they are hidden by each layered row **[figure 4]**.

9 Center punch and drill the marks for the tube rivets with a #42 drill bit. Center punch and drill the top of the tail piece.

10 Draw a beak design with permanent marker. Center punch and drill a hole at the starting point. Saw the beak detail in your found object. Drill the nostril detail carefully with the #42 drill bit, then file smooth.

11 Place the bottom row of feathers on the body piece. Use 1 hole in the feather row as a template and mark through the hole onto the body with the permanent marker. Center punch and drill the body hole.

12 Insert a piece of copper ³⁄₃₂" (2.3 mm) tubing through the hole in the feathers, the body, and the hole in the tail. Mark the tubing, leaving ¹⁄₃₂" (.79 mm) on the front and back. Cut the tubing with the jeweler's saw frame and #1/0 saw blade. Use the center punch, dapping tools, and ball-peen hammer to rivet the tube in place.

13 Mark the placement of the second hole on the body. Center punch, drill the hole, and measure the tubing, leaving 1–1.5 mm on either side of the piece. Cut 11 pieces of tubing to match. Mark the remaining holes, center punch, drill, and rivet.

14 Drill and rivet 1 hole at a time until all the feather rows are in place **[figure 5]**.

15 Use chain-nose pliers to bend the tabs 90 degrees, to fit the found object into place. Remove the found object.

16 Brush and clean the metal with a brass or satin brush. Oxidize the piece with liver of sulfur or Black Max. Rinse and dry completely. Use a brass brush or steel wool on the surfaces for the desired finish **[figure 6]**.

17 Set the found object using a prong pusher or burnishing tool. Bend side tabs first, then the top tabs, until the object is fully set in place.

Copper Pocket

DESIGNED BY:
Janice Berkebile

FINISHED SIZE:
1" wide x 1½" high
(2.5 cm x 3.8 cm)

A NEW TOOL AND THE EXPLORATION OF IT are always good inspiration! I was teaching etching, and the disc cutter and dapping block landed on my desk about the same time. I started to play with the disc cutter, using the etched metal, and the result is this fabulous Copper Pocket.

materials

3" x 3" (7.6 x 7.6 cm) of copper or sterling silver 24-gauge sheet

6" (15.2 cm) of sterling silver 18-gauge wire

5 sterling silver handmade 20-gauge 2" (5 cm) balled-end head pins (see spotlight)

2 lampworked 3–4mm beads

tools

Disc cutter

Metal shears

File or 180/100-grit emery board

Design and alphabet stamps

Utility hammer

Steel bench block and pad

Fine-tip permanent marker

Ruler or tape measure

1.8 mm metal hole-punch pliers

Dapping block and punches

Liver of sulfur or darkening agent

Pro-Polish polishing pad

Chasing hammer

Assorted texturing hammers

Pliers: chain-nose, round-nose, and flat-nose

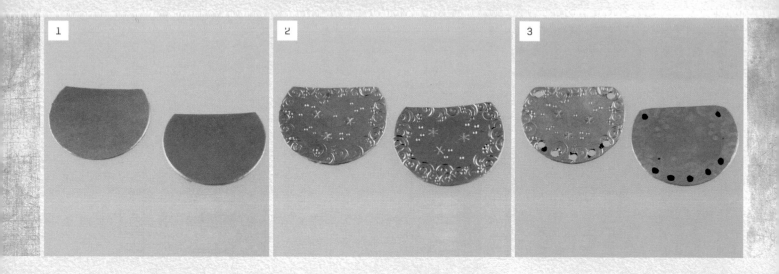

1 For each copper pocket cut out two 1" (2.5 cm) discs from the copper sheet using the disc cutter.

2 Trim the top off of 1 disc using the metal shears [figure 1].

3 Hold the second disc next to the first and trim the second to match.

4 File or sand the discs with a 180/100-grit emery board until the edges are smooth.

5 Create a border on one side of each disc by stamping around the edges, moving the stamp in and out and overlapping each stamp [figure 2].

6 Use a fine-tip marker to mark the front of one of the discs where the holes should be punched. Place all marks 1/16" (1.5 mm) from the edge. The first mark should be the center bottom, then make 2 marks on either side of the center. Make 1 mark on each side of the top.

7 Use the hole-punch pliers to punch out the holes in the first disc.

8 Position the discs inside to inside. Use the existing holes as a template to mark through the first disc to the second disc with a fine-point permanent marker [figure 3].

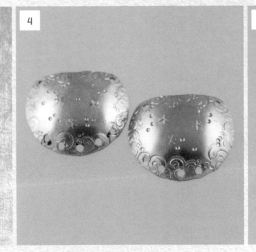

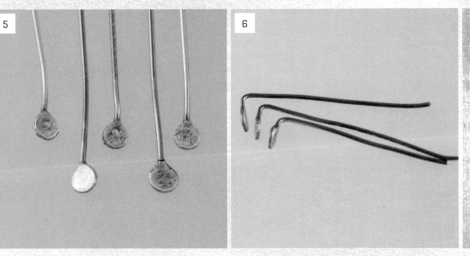

9 Punch out the holes of the second disc exactly as the holes are marked.

10 With the textured side facing down, dap the pieces using a shallow well. Dap gently so the holes do not stretch, but dap enough to get a smooth form [figure 4].

11 Dip the discs in a hot liver of sulfur solution; rinse and dry. Polish with a Pro-Polish pad.

12 Flatten the balls on 5 balled-end head pins with a chasing hammer. Texture or stamp the flattened balls [figure 5]. Add beads to 2 of the head pins.

13 Hold a beadless head pin with the tip of the chain-nose pliers above the flattened ball. Bend the wire toward you over the top of chain-nose pliers. Leave about 1/16" (1.5 mm) above the flattened ball [figure 6].

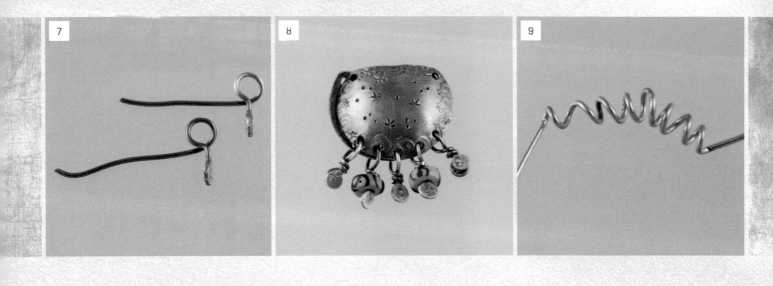

14 Hold the flattened ball from underneath and place the base of round-nose pliers on the wire. Rotate the round-nose pliers until a loop is created. Finish the loop form by wrapping with the other hand. Repeat with 2 beaded head pins and 2 plain head pins [figure 7].

15 Hold the domed copper pieces together and add a beadless flattened head pin to the center bottom. Slide the loop from the front of the dome to the back of the second piece to connect pocket halves.

16 Repeat on either side alternating beaded and beadless head pins. Each loop should be large enough for the pieces to move freely.

17 Grasp a beaded head pin with chain-nose pliers covering the loop. Tightly wrap the wire twice around directly under the loop. Trim off excess.

18 Grasp a beadless head pin the same way and wrap the wire around twice. Instead of trimming the excess, form a spiral; press to seat it to the back of the flattened ball [figure 8].

19 Mark the center of a 6" [15.2 cm] piece of 18-gauge sterling silver wire with permanent marker.

20 Grasp the wire with chain-nose pliers 1" [2.5 cm] in from the end. Using the tip of the pliers, vine the wire up until you reach the halfway mark. Repeat, starting 1" [2.5 cm] in from the other end [figure 9].

21 Insert one straight end of the spiraled wire through one of the top holes from the front to the back of the pocket. Insert the other end of the wire from the back to the front and spiral the ends with your chain-nose pliers. Lift or bend out the spirals and hammer to flatten. Press or seat the spirals against the domed pocket.

Sterling Silver Balled-end Head Pins

This technique involves the use of a simple butane micro-torch to melt a ball on the end of sterling silver wire. You can find these torches in any hardware store.

1   Set up over a noncombustible surface. Load your torch with butane and fill a small dish with water for quenching the hot head pins.

2   Cut ten 2" (5 cm) lengths of sterling silver 20-gauge wire.

3   Hold the tip of 1 piece of wire with the tweezers. Place the other end of the wire past the blue cone of the flame and allow the wire to ball up. At this point, the ball will want to drop. Stop, quench the wire in water, and place it on the table. Repeat.

materials

20-gauge sterling silver wire

tools

Flameproof work surface

Butane micro-torch

Butane

Metal or glass dish of water

Wire cutters

Long tweezers

TIP

You want the ball to be as big as possible, so allow it to ball up as far as it will go until it begins to quiver.

ALSO USED IN:
Garden Wind Gong Pendant, page 034
Gambler's Luck Necklace, page 120

Faux Bone Bracelet

DESIGNED BY:
Robert Dancik

FINISHED SIZE:
3³/₄" wide x 4¹/₄"high
[9.5 cm x 10.8 cm]

I'VE ALWAYS LIKED THE PHRASE "WEARING YOUR HEART ON YOUR SLEEVE" to describe the adoring feelings one might have for one's partner in love. I started thinking about the possibilities of this idea manifesting physically. I then thought that perhaps this could be so for any feeling—loving or otherwise. The lines on the front represent the thinking process while the words on the back are the conclusion reached.

materials

¹/₄" [6.3 mm] thick piece of Faux Bone sheet
Copper 22-gauge sheet
Copper 14-gauge wire
Image from any source

tools

Fine-point permanent marker
Circle templates
Ruler
Jeweler's saw frame
Special Faux Bone saw blades*
#2/0 saw blades
Bench pin
Drill or flex shaft
#52 drill bit
Faux Bone shaping tool*
Texturing tools

Bench block
Center punch
Half-round file, #2 cut
Silicon carbide [wet/dry] sandpaper in 320-, 400-, and 600 grit
Liver of sulfur or patina
Wire cutters
¹/₈" [3.1 mm] drill bit
Electric engraver, scribes, rotary grinding/polishing tools, carving tools
Checkering file
Scissors
PVA glue
Burnt umber acrylic paint
Craft knife
Brown shoe polish or wax
Round-faced hammer
Epoxy resin
Toothpick

*available at www.fauxbone.com

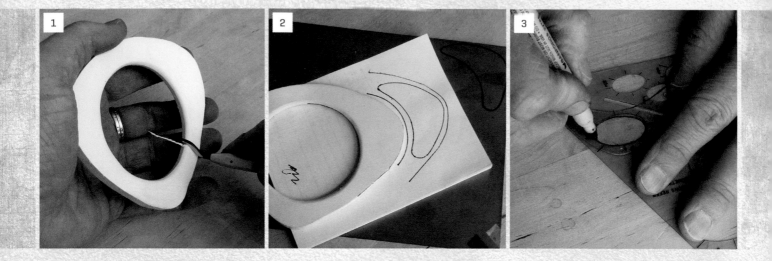

1   Draw the shape of the opening for your bracelet (round, square, or otherwise) on a piece of ¼" (6.3 mm) thick Faux Bone sheet. The minimum diameter for a bracelet opening is 2⅝" (6.6 cm). Draw the outside shape of the bracelet, making sure to leave enough room for your copper appliqué in Step 2, and leaving at least ¼" (6.3 mm) between the outside and inside shapes. *(Optional: Use a precut Faux Bone bracelet blank.)*

2   Use the jeweler's saw frame and a special Faux Bone blade to cut out the outside shape. Drill a small hole with the #52 drill bit just inside the inside shape and saw out the inside. Smooth and round the edges of the opening with the half-round file or a Faux Bone shaping tool **[figure 1]**.

3   Place the bracelet on a sheet of paper and with a permanent marker, trace around the portion of the bracelet where the copper appliqué will sit. Remove the bracelet and with a permanent marker, transfer the drawing to the copper 22-gauge sheet. If you are going to texture the copper, now is the time to do so—before you begin to cut it **[figure 2]**.

4   Use an oval circle template to draw an inside window shape on the copper appliqué for your image **[figure 3]**.

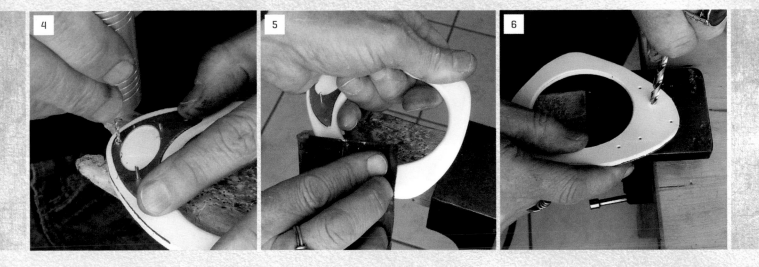

5 Plan where the rivets will go to hold the appliqué to the bracelet. Center punch and drill holes in the copper appliqué with a #52 drill bit.

6 Drill a small hole just inside the center opening shape in the copper appliqué and saw out the inside shape using a #2/0 saw blade. Saw the outside shape. File, sand, and patina the copper as desired with heat and or chemicals.

7 Place the copper appliqué on the Faux Bone bracelet where it will ultimately sit. Using the rivet holes as a guide, drill 1 hole in the Faux Bone and insert a piece of 14-gauge wire into that hole to keep its place. Drill the next hole and insert another wire to hold that place. Once you have 2 wires in place, you can drill all the rest of the holes [figure 4].

8 With the copper appliqué in place, shape and smooth the outside of the bracelet with files or on a small belt sander [figure 5].

9 Remove the copper appliqué. Using a ⅛" (3.1 mm) drill bit in your hand, lightly twist the drill bit to countersink the top of the holes in the copper appliqué and the bottom of the holes in the Faux Bone. This will allow the rivet heads to sit in the copper more neatly, and become almost flush with the Faux Bone surface [figure 6].

10 Sand the bracelet all over with silicon carbide (wet/dry) sandpaper, using lots of water to speed the process and make the surface smoother. Start with 320-grit, proceed with 400-grit, and finish with 600-grit.

11 Draw any design on the Faux Bone bracelet with a fine-tip permanent marker. I decided on simple lines on the copper appliqué side and words on the other. Incise these marks into the Faux Bone using tools such as an electric engraver, carving tools, scribes, rotary carving bits on a flex shaft or similar machine, or any other tool that will work to mark the surface.

TIP

It's important to keep the copper appliqué in place so that you don't remove too much material from the bracelet.

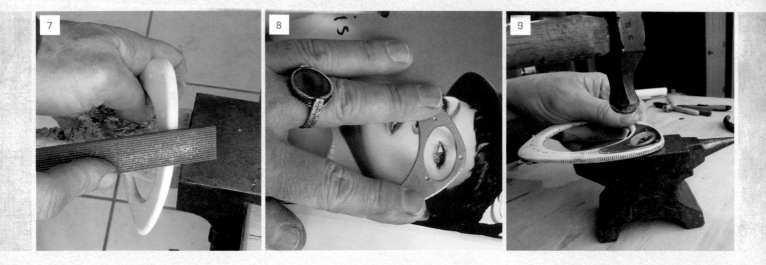

12 Use these same tools to make any marks you like on the Faux Bone. I used a checkering file to incise lines on the edge of the bracelet **[figure 7]**.

13 Sand again with 600-grit sandpaper to remove any burrs that might have risen on the surface. Then, turn the 600-grit sandpaper over on the paper side and, using water, rub the bracelet vigorously with the back of the sandpaper. This will give a lovely soft sheen to the Faux Bone. Or, the bracelet can be buffed on a polishing wheel using a small loose-sewn plain muslin buff with no compound.

14 Use the copper appliqué to go "image mining" by moving the center hole over images, words, etc., until you find the image you want for your bracelet. Trace the outside of the copper appliqué on the image. Remove the appliqué and draw another line on the image, just inside the previous line; cut out the image. Seal both sides of the image with PVA glue, let dry, and then glue the image to the back of the copper appliqué with the image facing out **[figure 8]**.

15 Rub burnt umber acrylic paint into the incised lines on the bracelet and let it dry for just a moment, then rub it off, leaving it in the lines. Remove as much or as little paint as you like using the 600-grit sandpaper. I also scratched the surface of the bracelet with the sharp edge of a craft knife to make what will look like craze marks on the surface, also adding to the look of age in the piece.

16 Apply a very thin coat of shoe polish or wax to the bracelet (I used brown polish, again, for the aging effect) and allow to dry. Buff to a soft sheen.

17 Rivet the frame to the bracelet with 14-gauge copper wire **[figure 9]**.

18 Place the bracelet on a level surface where you won't have to move it and float a thin coat of resin over the image in the frame (see Resin Spotlight). Fill it slowly, until the resin flows to the edge of the copper cutout and just begins to dome. Allow to set and cure for 24 hours before touching the bracelet.

TIP

Make sure to insert all the rivet wires before you begin to rivet any of them. The rivet heads on the back of the bracelet should sit nicely into the countersunk holes.

Resin

1 Trace the outside of a coin twice on a piece of white paper, leaving about ½" (1.2 cm) between the 2 circles. Place a piece of waxed paper on top of the circles. Squeeze a small amount of the resin part A into 1 circle and repeat for part B into the second circle.

2 With a scrap of wire or a palette knife, combine the two parts and mix the resin gently and thoroughly.

3 When mixed, breathe on the resin several times; the warmth of your breath will thin the resin slightly, allowing the bubbles to get to the surface easier and also make it easier to spread in the copper appliqué well.

4 Scoop up a bit of the resin and let it drip onto the center of the image. It will start to spread on its own, and breathing on it again will help this process. Keep adding resin and use a toothpick to push it to the edge of the copper appliqué until it flows evenly to the edges and begins to dome up slightly [figure 1].

5 Place the piece on a level surface (a bowl of rice grains is a good place to level the bracelet) and allow to cure for 24 hours.

TIP

Take care not to whip it up or you will make bubbles that will cloud the resin. If you use a longer setting resin (20 minutes or so), the bubbles have a better chance to migrate to the surface and not be trapped in the resin.

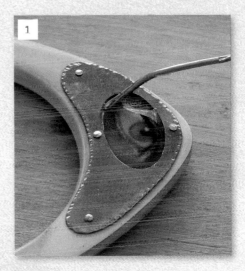

Cold Fusion Necklace

DESIGNED BY:
Connie Fox

FINISHED SIZE:
31" (79 cm) long

I NEVER MET A COLD CONNECTION I DIDN'T LOVE—
but I definitely love some more than others. Wire and tube
rivets, miniature bolts, and the mesh screen you see in this
fabulous necklace top the list. This necklace fuses brass,
copper, and silver into a piece that is sure to garner attention.

materials

20-gauge metal sheet in sterling silver, copper,
and brass

16-gauge dead-soft round sterling silver and
copper wire

16-gauge dead-soft half-round sterling silver
wire

Manufactured metal blanks (shapes):

- Copper 18-gauge: one 1¾" x ½" (4.4cm
  x 1.2 cm) oval, and one ¾" x ¾" (1.9cm)
  square
- Copper 20-gauge round: one ¾" (1.9cm),
  one 1" (2.5cm), two 1¼" (3.1cm)
- Copper 24-gauge round: one ⅜" (9.2mm)
- Sterling silver 22-gauge round: five 1"
  (2.5cm)
- Sterling silver 24-gauge round: four ½"
  (1.2cm), one ¾" (1.9cm)
- Brass washers, 24-gauge: two ¾" (1.9cm)

Copper mesh

7 brass hex bolts, washers, nuts: #0-80, ¼"
(6.3 mm) long

1 brass fillister bolt, washer, nut: #0-80, ¼"
(6.3 mm) long

Brass tubing: ⅛" (3.1 mm) diameter

Copper tubing: ³/₃₂" (2.3 mm) diameter

Sterling silver tubing: .1141" (2.9 mm)
diameter dead-soft tubing

Manufactured brass flat-head tubing

Brass eyelet

Image

Plastic sheet protector

Clay

Beads: 1 lampworked disc and 1 small bead to
use as a washer

Jump rings

tools

Fine-tip permanent marker

Circle template

Ruler

Jeweler's saw frame

#2/0 and #5/0 saw blades

Lubricant: beeswax, Bur Life or Cut Lube

Drill or flex shaft

Set of twist drill bits

Twist drill bits: #42, #53, and #55

Half-round flat file, #2 cut

Texture tools: metal stamps, nail sets,
hammers

Anvil

Round-nose, chain-nose, and flat-nose pliers

Center punch

Flush cutters

Riveting hammer

Dapping set

Liver of sulfur (optional)

Scissors

Ring clamp

2 miniature wrenches

Clear nail polish

Twist drill gauge

Micro torch

Cross-lock tweezers

Bowl of water

Pickle or Pro-Polish polishing pad

Bench pin

Universal eyelet setter

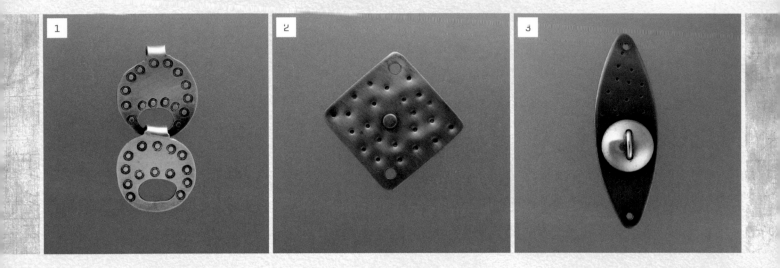

1 TWO SILVER DISCS WITH TABS

Draw two 18 mm circles each with a 5 x 9 mm tab on the 20-gauge sterling silver sheet. Draw one 5 x 8 mm hole on each disc, 2.5 mm from the edge opposite the tab. Use the jeweler's saw frame and #2/0 saw blade to cut out the discs. For the inside hole, drill a small pilot hole first just inside the hole outline, then saw out the shape. File the edges, then stamp with a nail set to decorate. Lace one tab through the hole in the other disc and bend the tab into a loop with the tips of round-nose pliers to connect the 2 pieces. Bend another loop in the remaining tab [figure 1].

2 BRASS SQUARE TEXTURE

Draw a 20 mm square on brass 20-gauge sheet. Use the jeweler's saw frame and #2/0 saw blade to cut out the square. File the edges smooth and round the corners. Texture the square with a center punch. Drill a hole in the center of the square with a #55 drill bit. Make a rivet with 16-gauge copper wire. Make 2 other holes to attach the square to the necklace with jump rings [figure 2].

3 SILVER STAPLE ON DAPPED DISC

Use the copper 18-gauge 1¾" x ½" (4.4 x 1.2cm) oval blank. Use a center punch to texture one side of the copper oval. Use a sterling silver 24-gauge ½" (12.7mm) disc blank. Drill 2 holes 6 mm apart in the disc with a #55 drill bit. Dap the disc in the dapping block to dome. Center the disc on the copper oval piece and use the holes in the disc to drill matching holes in the copper oval. Bend a piece of 1½" (3.8 cm) sterling silver 16-gauge round wire to form a staple. Insert the wire in the holes on the disc, dome-side first, pass through the holes in the copper oval. Trim the ends so they are even, then spread the wires and use round-nose pliers to make small loops on the ends. Press the wires flat against the back of the copper oval. Drill 2 additional holes for your jump rings [figure 3].

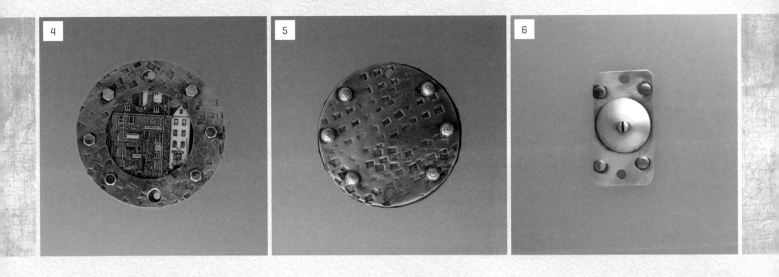

TIP

If you are going to add a patina,
do it prior to bolting.

4 CAPTURED PICTURE WITH BOLTS

Use 2 copper 20-gauge 1¼" (3.1cm) disc blanks. Texture the discs with your texturing tools. Mark a circle in the middle of one blank; make allowance for a ¼" (6.3 mm) frame. Drill a pilot hole, drill, saw and file. The "top" piece has the window to view the image; the bottom piece is solid. Use a #53 drill bit to drill 6 holes in the top piece where you will connect the top and bottom together and 2 additional holes for your jump rings. Cut your image and plastic sheet protector slightly smaller than the top disc size. Sandwich the image and sheet protector between both pieces of metal; secure tightly in a ring clamp and drill through all layers. Use six #0-80, ¼" (6.3 mm) hex bolts to thread through all the layers (bolt head on top). Add the washers and, with two miniature wrenches, secure the nuts. Saw off the ends of the bolts and file flush with the nuts [figures 4 and 5]. Use a small amount of clear nail polish on the back of each bolt to secure them.

5 TELESCOPING BOLT INSIDE SILVER DAPPED DISC

Draw a 13.5 x 26 mm rectangle on sterling silver 20-gauge sheet. Use the jeweler's saw frame and #2/0 saw blade to cut out the rectangle. File the edges and round the corners. Drill 4 holes in the rectangle with a #55 drill bit. Make 4 copper 16-gauge wire rivets in the rectangle. Use 1 sterling silver 24-gauge ½" (1.2cm) disc blank and drill a center hole through the disc with #53 drill bit. Place the disc over the rectangle and drill through the first hole and the rectangle. Dap the silver disc into a dome shape. Attach the disc to the rectangle with a brass #0-80, ¼" (6.3 mm) fillister bolt, washer, and nut. Saw off the end of the bolt and rivet the end [figure 6].

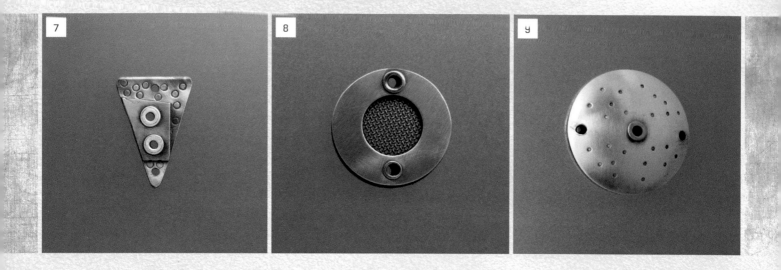

6 TUBE-RIVETED BRASS TRIANGLE

Draw a 17 x 26 x 26 mm triangle on the brass 20-gauge sheet. Use the jeweler's saw frame and #2/0 saw blade to cut out the triangle. File the edges and round corners. Use the nail set to texture the brass. Saw out a piece of copper 20-gauge sheet that will fit on top of the triangle shape; file the edges. Measure the shank of the sterling silver tubing by placing it in the drill gauge to determine what size drill bit is needed. Drill 2 holes in the copper shape. Place the copper shape on top of the brass triangle; drill through the holes in the copper, through the brass. Make 2 sterling silver tube rivets to connect the copper piece to the brass triangle. Drill 2 holes for your jump rings [figure 7].

7 BRASS WASHERS AND CAPTURED SCREEN

Use two ¾" (1.9cm) brass 24-gauge washers. Use a #42 drill bit to drill 2 holes opposite each other on 1 washer; this will be the "top" washer. Cut a piece of copper mesh that is a little smaller than ¾" round and sandwich it between the top washer and a second washer. Secure the 2 washers tightly in a ring clamp. Drill through the first holes, mesh disc, and bottom washer. Make 2 copper ³/₃₂" diameter (.014") tube rivets to hold the pieces together [figure 8].

8 LENTIL BEAD WITH TELESCOPING TUBE RIVET

Use 2 sterling silver 22-gauge 1" (2.5cm) disc blanks. Texture each disc with a center punch. Use a #53 drill bit to drill a pilot hole in the center of 1 disc. In a ring clamp, secure the drilled disc on top of the other disc and drill the second hole. Drill 1 hole on each side, opposite each other, on 1 disc (for your jump rings). Use the ring clamp to secure the 2 discs and drill through the top hole on one side and then through the bottom disc; repeat for the other side. Use a dapping set to form both discs into domes that will form a lentil shape when together. Drill both center holes with a #42 drill bit. To prevent the tubing from collapsing as you hammer, use a larger, close-fitting brass ⅛" (3.1 mm) diameter tubing to sleeve the smaller copper ³/₃₂" (2.3 mm) tubing. The sleeved section will be

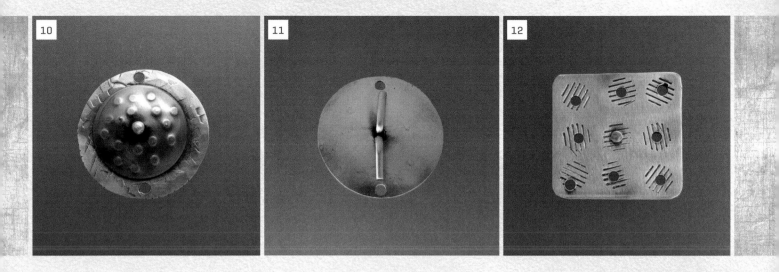

TIP

Make the sleeve just a little shorter than this measurement

note

This component should only be made if you are familiar with a handheld torch and use good safety practices.

inside the lentil bead. Determine the length of the sleeve by placing the 3/32" (2.3 mm) tubing in one hole, wrap it with clay, place the other end of the lentil bead through the tubing. Press together. The clay will be sandwiched between the domes and the height of the clay is the length of your sleeve. Slip the sleeve onto the 3/32" (2.3 mm) tubing in this order: 1 dome of the lentil bead, the 1/8" (3.1 mm) diameter tubing sleeve, the other dome of the lentil bead. Rivet the tube to hold the pieces together **[figure 9]**.

9   BALL STAPLE
Use 1 sterling silver 22-gauge 1" (2.5cm) disc blank and 1 copper 20-gauge 3/4" (1.9cm) disc blank. Texture the silver disc with a texture hammer. Texture the copper disc with a nail set. Drill the center of the copper disc with a #55 drill bit. Place the copper disc on top of the silver disc and drill through the first hole and bottom disc. Dap the copper disc into a dome. Fold 2½" (6.3 cm) of sterling silver 16-gauge half-round wire in half with the rounded sides together. Hold the ends of the wire in cross-lock tweezers and form a ball with the torch on the end of the fold. Quench the wire in a bowl of water to cool. Pickle and clean or use a Pro-Polish polishing pad to remove the excess oxidation. Thread the wire through the holes in the copper and silver piece and spread the wires to form a staple. Drill 2 holes with a #53 drill bit on each side of the silver disc, opposite each other, for your jump rings **[figures 10 and 11]**.

10 SILVER SQUARE WITH HOLES
Draw a 26 x 26 mm square on the sterling silver 20-gauge sheet. Use the jeweler's saw frame and #2/0 saw blade to cut out the square. File the edges and round the corners. Use a design stamp to texture the square in a pattern that pleases you. Use a #55 drill bit to pierce the pattern. Make a copper 16-gauge wire rivet in one of the holes **[figure 12]**.

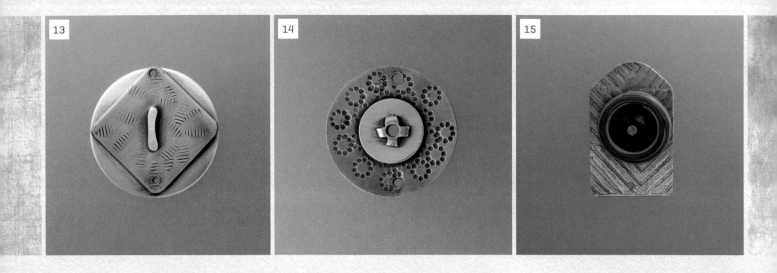

11 SILVER STAPLE

Use 1 sterling silver 22-gauge 1" (2.5cm) disc blank and 1 copper 18-gauge ¾" x ¾" (1.9 x 1.9cm) square blank. Texture the copper square with a design stamp. Drill 2 holes in the copper square with a #55 drill bit. Place the copper square over the silver disc; secure in a ring clamp. Drill through the first 2 holes, through the silver disc. Form a staple with sterling silver 16-gauge round wire that fits through the holes. On the back of the silver disc, trim the wire and rivet the ends. Drill 2 holes for your jump rings [figure 13].

12 SPLIT-TUBE RIVET

Use a copper 20-gauge 1" (2.5cm) disc blank and a sterling silver 24-gauge ½" (1.2cm) disc blank. Texture the copper disc with a design stamp. Drill a hole in the middle of the silver disc with a #42 drill bit. Place the silver disc on the copper disc and drill through the first hole, through the copper disc. Mark 4 points of a cross on the end of a piece of brass ³/₃₂" (2.3 mm) diameter tubing. Mark the circumference of the tubing 3mm down from the end to indicate the stop line for sawing. Using a jeweler's saw frame and #5/0 saw blade, with your tubing secured in the "V" of a bench pin, saw on the cross-hatch marks down to the 3mm mark. Use chain-nose pliers to fold down the four ends of the cross. Place the tubing into the hole and finish the back as a standard tube rivet. Drill 2 holes for your jump rings [figure 14].

13 BRASS BOLT WITH GLASS BEADS

Draw a 20 x 33 mm rectangle with one rounded end on brass 20-gauge sheet. Use a jeweler's saw and #2/0 saw blade to cut out the shape. File the edges. Texture the brass shape with a texture hammer. Drill a hole in the brass sheet using a #53 drill bit. Use a #0-80, ¼" (6.35mm) long miniature hex bolt to attach a glass disc and a small glass bead as a washer to the front of the brass shape. Use a small brass washer and a nut on the reverse side to secure the beads to the brass. Use 2 miniature wrenches to carefully tighten the bolt. Saw off the end of the bolt. Use a flex shaft or a file to smooth the end of the bolt [figure 15]. Use clear nail polish on the nut to secure the bolt. Drill 2 holes for your jump rings.

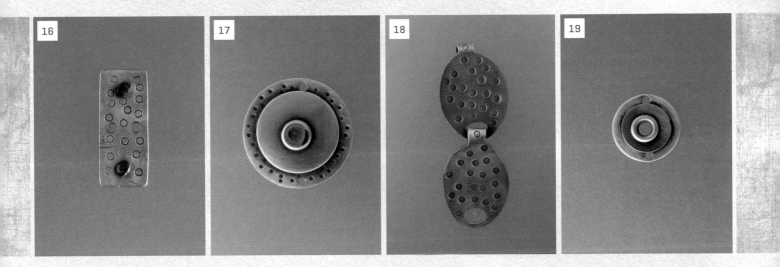

14 SILVER RECTANGLE WITH TWO COPPER RIVETS

Draw a 10 x 25 mm rectangle on sterling silver 20-gauge sheet. Use a jeweler's saw and #2/0 saw blade to cut out the shape. File the edges and round the corners. Stamp with a nail set. Drill 2 holes with a #53 drill bit on either end of the rectangle. Drill 2 holes for your jump rings. Make 2 copper rivets with copper 16-gauge round wire [figure 16].

15 MANUFACTURED TUBE RIVET

Use 1 sterling silver 22-gauge 1" (2.5cm) disc blank and 1 sterling silver 24-gauge ³⁄₄" (1.9cm) disc blank. Texture the large disc with a center punch. Measure the shank of the manufactured brass flat-head tubing by placing it in the drill gauge; this will determine what size drill bit is needed. Drill a hole in the small disc. Place the small disc over the larger disc, insert into a ring clamp and drill through both discs. Rivet the flat-head tubing to connect the pieces together. Drill 2 holes for your jump rings [figure 17].

16 TWO COPPER OVALS WITH TABS

Draw two 18 x 25 mm ovals with 5 x 9 mm tabs on copper 20-gauge sheet. Use a jeweler's saw and #2/0 saw blade to cut out the shapes. File the edges. Decorate the pieces with a nail set. Saw a 5 x 7 mm hole in each piece, 2 mm from the edge. Lace one tab through the hole of the other piece and bend the tab into a loop with the tips of round-nose pliers. Make a loop with the remaining tab [figure 18].

17 BRASS EYELET WITH SMALL COPPER AND SILVER DISCS

Use 1 sterling silver 24-gauge ½" (1.2cm) disc blank and 1 copper 24-gauge ³⁄₈" (9.5mm) disc blank. In the drill gauge, measure the shank of a brass eyelet to determine the drill bit size. Drill a hole in the copper disc. Place the copper disc on top of the silver disc; drill through the first hole and through the silver disc. Place a brass eyelet through the hole and use the universal eyelet setter to secure the eyelet. Drill 2 holes for your jump rings [figure 19].

note

If the shank has a large diameter, make sure you drill several pilot holes leading up to the final large drill bit.

TIP

Eyelets can be used with care as cold connections. Many of them are thin plated base metal. They split easily, and the plating can wear off. To prevent splitting, use an eyelet setter cautiously to form the tube.

Double-sided Pendant

DESIGNED BY:
Lisa Niven-Kelly

FINISHED SIZE:
10½" long x 1⅝" wide

I HAVE ALWAYS LOVED THE LOOK OF MIXED METALS.

To me, there is something casual about sterling silver and
something a bit more fancy about gold. With this necklace,
you get two looks in one piece. Wear it comfortably with jeans,
then flip it when you are ready for your night at the opera.

materials

1 sterling silver 1½" x ¾" (3.8 x 1.9cm) oval washer

1 gold-filled 1½" x ¾" (3.8 x 1.9cm) oval washer

1 sterling silver ⅞" (2.2cm) square washer with a ½" (1.2cm) ID (inner diameter)

1 gold-filled ⅞" (2.2cm) square washer with a ½" (1.2cm) ID

2" (5 cm) of sterling silver thin-walled tubing: 1.5 mm ID, 2 mm OD

2" (5 cm) of sterling silver 16-gauge round wire

2 sterling silver 14-gauge 8mm ID jump rings

16" (40.6 cm) of sterling silver or gold-filled chain

Sterling silver or gold-filled clasp

tools

Steel bench block

Fretz texturing hammers

Chasing hammer

Design stamps: bull's eye, parentheses, period, and bubble

16-ounce brass-head hammer

Liver of sulfur

Pro-Polish polishing pad

Fine-tip permanent marker

Ruler

1.25 mm hole-punch pliers

Round fine-tip file

Jeweler's saw frame

#2/0 saw blades

Flush cutters

Riveting hammer

Nylon-jaw pliers

2 chain-nose pliers

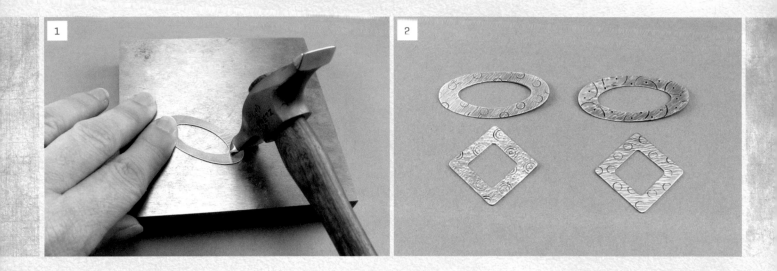

TIP

If texturing with a design stamp, use a 16-ounce brass-head hammer to make the impression.

TIP

Sometimes hole-punch pliers can mar the metal around the hole. Try sandwiching a thick piece of paper between the tool and the washer to cushion it a bit.

1 Place the washers on a steel bench block and texture by either striking them in a pattern with a texture hammer or by stamping them with a design stamp **[figure 1]**.

2 Patina the washers with liver of sulfur, then use a Pro-Polish pad to polish and bring out the texturing detail **[figure 2]**.

3 Using a permanent marker, mark the riveting placement holes in each sterling washer; center the holes at the top, bottom, left, and right of the washer, each 2 mm inside the edge.

4 Punch the holes in the sterling washers with 1.25 mm hole-punch pliers **[figure 3]**.

5 Line up the oval sterling silver washers with the matching gold-filled washers, with the textured sides facing out. Using the hole-punch, punch through the holes in the sterling silver washers into the gold-filled washers. Repeat with the square washers.

6 Ream out the holes with a round tip file on all 4 washers to prepare them for riveting. The 16-gauge rivet wire should fit tightly.

7 Use a jeweler's saw frame and #2/0 blade to cut four 2 mm pieces of sterling silver tubing. The tubing will be used as "spacers" between the top and bottom rivets of both sets of shapes.

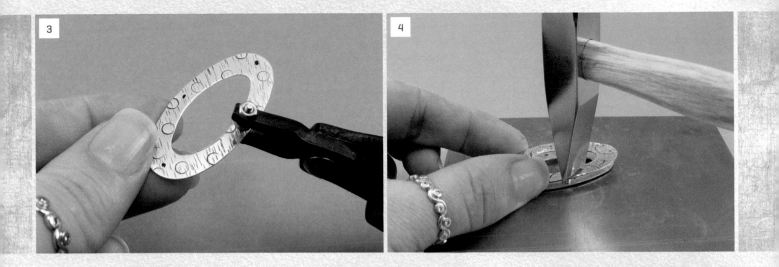

TIP

Use your nondominant hand to brace and hold up the side that you are not riveting to keep it from collapsing

8   Thread the sterling silver 16-gauge wire through the top hole on the front of the sterling silver oval washer, through one 2 mm tube piece, and the top hole on the back side of the gold-filled washer. This will form a silver and gold "sandwich" with the textured sides of the washers facing out.

9   Using wire cutters, trim the 16-gauge wire, leaving 1 mm on either side of the "sandwich." Using the riveting hammer, rivet the wire in place [figure 4].

10 Repeat Steps 8 and 9 to rivet the bottom holes.

11 Use nylon-jaw pliers to pinch down and hold together the 2 holes on the left of the oval washers. Insert the 16-gauge wire through both holes and trim the wire, leaving 1 mm on either side. Rivet the wire in place.

12 Repeat Step 11 for the holes on the right side.

13 Repeat Steps 8–12 with the square washers.

14 Connect the 2 pieces together. Open one 8mm jump ring and loop it around the tubed rivet on the bottom of the oval piece and the tubed rivet on the top of the square piece. Close the jump ring.

15 Open another 8mm jump ring and close it around the tubed rivet on the top of the oval piece. Attach two sides of a chain or add another jump ring as a bale and thread a chain through that jump ring.

Poker Chip Brooch

DESIGNED BY:
Marthe Roberts-Shea

FINISHED SIZE:
3¼" long x 2¼" wide
(8.26 cm x 5.72 cm)

POKER CHIPS ARE IN ABUNDANCE. Some of the older chips are so beautifully illustrated or are so graphically appealing that it seems a shame to just restrict them to the card game. I saw this chip and had to own it. The pin part of the brooch acts as a fulcrum from which the corrugated "petals" are attached, giving the brooch lots of movement.

materials

4½" x 4½" (11.4 x 11.4 cm) of sterling silver 24-gauge sheet

4½" (11.4 cm) of sterling silver 18-gauge wire

1.8 mm OD and 1.3 mm ID sterling silver tubing (about 14 gauge)

1 poker chip

One 14K gold pearl peg (hoop charm earring component)

1 half-drilled 6 or 8mm round or teardrop-shaped pearl

1 oxidized sterling silver grooved 12mm closed ring

tools

Flush cutters

Vise

Draw tongs

Fine-tip permanent marker

Jeweler's saw frame

#2 saw blades

Tube-cutting jig

Round bezel mandrel

Rawhide mallet

Half-round file, #2 cut

ZAM polish

Small anvil or steel bench block

Bench pin

Circle template

Industrial tube wringer

Metal scribe

Flex shaft

#60 (1 mm) drill bit

T-pins

Assorted needle files (including triangle)

Liver of sulfur

Goldsmith's hammer or riveting hammer

Parallel pliers

Half-round pliers

Quick-setting epoxy

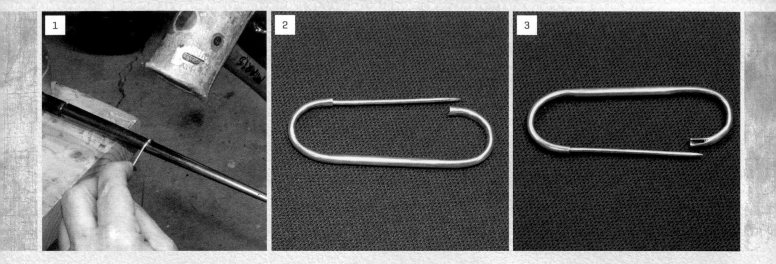

1   Cut 3½" [8.8 cm] of sterling silver 18-gauge wire. Straighten it by putting one end of the wire in a vise and the other end in the jaws of a draw tong. Pull the wire until it's straightened.

2   Use the fine-tip permanent marker to mark the tubing at 2½" [6.3 cm] length. Cut the tubing to the marked length using the jeweler's saw frame, #2 saw blade, and a tube-cutting jig.

3   Slide the sterling silver wire about ⅔ of the way into the tubing. The remaining ⅓ needs to be hollow, to act as a catch when the pin is completed.

4   Place one end of the tubing with the inserted wire over the bezel mandrel and hammer gently with the rawhide mallet. Be careful not to hit the tubing too aggressively. The object is to not crush the tubing but rather form it around the mandrel in a "U" shape [figure 1].

5   Double check to make sure that the wire is still ⅔ of the way into the tubing. Using the same technique, form the second "U" bend in the tubing; this bend should be opposite to the first bend [figure 2].

6   When both ends of the tubing are formed, cut the remaining wire down to slightly overlap the opposite side of the tubing. Using the half-round #2 file, shape the wire to a point and polish with ZAM polish until the point is smooth. Work-harden the point by placing it on the steel bench block and gently tapping it with a rawhide mallet.

7   Place the piece on a bench pin and saw a tiny slit in the hollow end of the tubing. The slit should be just wide enough to fit the pointed end of the wire [figure 3].

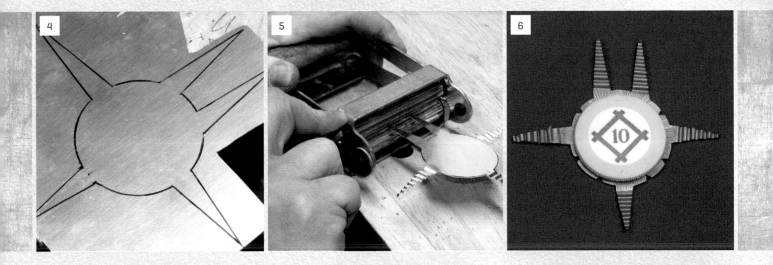

8   Use the marker and circle template to draw a circle with 5 points on the sterling silver 24-gauge sheet. Two of the points should be parallel to one another. These are going to be the parts that hook over the pin that you just completed [figure 4].

9   Cut the template out with a jeweler's saw.

10 Place the points of the sterling silver sheet in the industrial tube wringer. Press the tube wringer and turn the knob to corrugate each point. The two parallel points can be put through the wringer at the same time [figure 5].

11 Take the poker chip and use a scribe to mark the rivet placement at 6:00 and 12:00. Press firmly (be careful, some poker chips can be brittle) so that you can see a visible indentation. This indentation will act as a guide for the drill bit. Using the #60 drill bit, hold the poker chip firmly and run the drill at a slow speed while you drill the holes.

12 Center the poker chip on the sterling silver sheet. Place the T-pins through the drilled holes and press down on the pins to mark the silver sheet beneath. Drill a hole where the pins have left a mark with the #60 drill bit.

13 File V-shaped notches with the triangle needle file between the corrugated shapes for visual interest. File to smooth the holes and edges.

14 Dip the front and the corrugated points in liver of sulfur to blacken; rinse with water and dry.

15 Use a scribe to mark a "starburst" pattern on the front of the blackened sheet silver.

16 Rivet the poker chip to the drilled silver sheet with leftover sterling silver 18-gauge wire [figure 6].

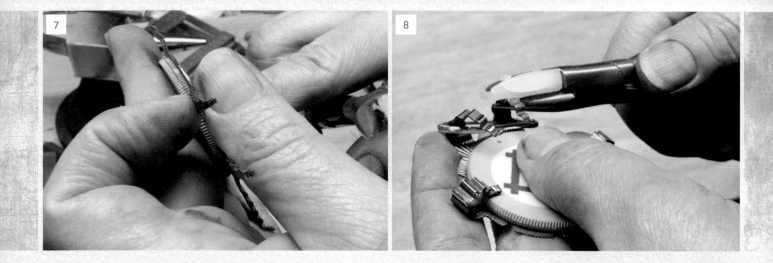

17 Use parallel pliers to bend over the very tips of the corrugated points. This will help eliminate any sharp points that can hurt somebody. Then, use half-round pliers to bend the tips of the corrugated points toward the back of the brooch [figure 7].

18 Use half-round pliers to grip the base of each of the corrugated points and bend them over the poker chip. Leave a little bit of space between the poker chip and the top 2 parallel pieces to slip in the pin part of the brooch. You will also need some space to slip the grooved 12mm ring through the bottom of the brooch.

19 Slip the top points through the bottom bar of the pin [figure 8].

20 Epoxy the pearl peg into the pearl and let the glue set. Saw one side of the grooved 12mm ring to split it like a jump ring.

21 Once the epoxy has set, insert the grooved 12mm ring through the pearl peg ring and make sure that the ends are flush to one another.

22 Insert the grooved 12mm ring, with the pearl peg attached, through the partially bent bottom corrugated point of the brooch. Bend the point the rest of the way onto the poker chip.

Work-hardening

The term "work-hardening" refers to the reaction metal has to being moved or manipulated. You can squeeze, bend, hammer, or pull metal through a series of successively smaller holes in a drawplate to "harden" the material. The stronger or "harder" the metals structure is, the more likely it will be to hold its shape. The crystal structure of the metal changes as you manipulate the metal. The more you work with it, the harder and more brittle it gets. Annealing or heating silver wire will relax and return the microscopic structure back to it's original soft state. In short, the more you bend wire or hammer it, the more brittle (or harder) it becomes. You can use a rawhide mallet and a steel bench block to hammer your wire or start with a thicker wire and draw (or reduce) it to a smaller gauge through a drawplate. You'll notice the material becomes stiffer the more you work it. Tumbling wire in a tumbler will work-harden the surface structure of it as well. The shot material acts like little hammers and helps to harden metal.

ALSO USED IN:
Fold-formed Leaf Bracelet, page 046

Hinged Bracelet

DESIGNED BY:
Richard Salley

FINISHED SIZE:
**1⅝" wide x 3" high
(4.13 cm x 7.62 cm)**

ONE OF THE THINGS THAT I ENJOY MOST about working in the genre of "found object" jewelry is to take something that we see or use on a daily basis and incorporate it into a piece of wearable art. For this project, I used a metal jar lid as a starting point. This bracelet was an opportunity to come up with a way of incorporating the jar lid into a hinged bracelet. I think the simple hinge and catch on this bracelet is both functional and elegant.

materials

1 distressed 43mm jar lid (Snapple lid)

Strip of copper 24-gauge sheet: ½" (1.2 cm) wide x jar lid diameter + 1" (2.5 cm)

1" x 5½" (2.5 x 13.9 cm) of copper 24-gauge sheet (length depends on wrist size)

6 solid brass #18 x ½" (1.2 cm) escutcheon pins

4" (10.1 cm) of copper 14-gauge wire

10' (3 m) of copper 20-gauge wire

1 focal piece: mineral specimen, rock, or other found object

tools

Texturing hammers or rolling mill

Steel bench block

Fine-tip permanent marker

Center punch

Ball-peen hammer

1.25 mm hole-punch pliers or drill and #56 drill bit

Flush cutters

Riveting hammer

Round-nose pliers

5-minute epoxy

Chasing hammer

Flat-nose pliers

Liver of sulfur

Pro-Polish polishing pad

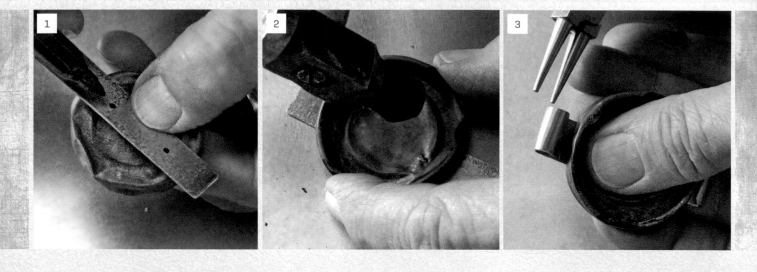

1 Using texturing hammers or a rolling mill, texture both pieces of copper sheet any way you like. I layered my sheet with a corn husk used in tamales and ran them through a rolling mill.

2 Hold the smaller strip of copper against the middle of the back of the jar lid so ¼" (6.3 mm) of the strip extends beyond the lid on one side, and ¾" (1.9 cm) extends beyond the lid on the other side. Using a fine-tip marker, mark 2 rivet hole locations inside the diameter of the jar lid. [figure 1].

3 Holding the strip in place and using the marks as a guide, center punch and drill the holes with a #56 drill bit, or use 1.25 mm hole-punch pliers.

4 Insert 2 escutcheon pins through the holes in the copper strip and the back of the lid. Turn the lid over and trim the pins, leaving just enough to form a rivet. Rivet the copper strip in place [figure 2].

5 Use round-nose pliers to curl the short end of the strip toward the inside of the lid but don't close the loop all the way. This will serve as the hinge on which the bracelet will rotate. Form a similar, slightly larger curl on the longer end of the strip; this will serve as the clasp [figure 3].

6 Create a nest-like coil of wire with the 20-gauge wire and press the coil into the jar lid under the lid tabs. If necessary, bend the lid slightly to hold the wire nest in place. Be sure to leave room in the middle for your focal object [figure 4].

7 Mix a small amount of 5-minute epoxy and put it into the center of the lid. Place your focal object in the epoxy inside the lid and set aside [figure 5].

8 Cut the 14-gauge wire in half. Form a U-shape with each wire that is slightly wider than the copper strip that has been riveted to the jar lid [figure 6].

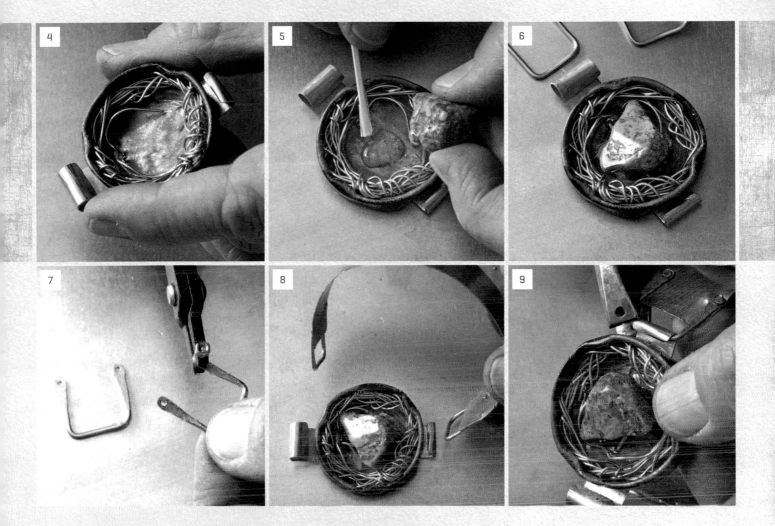

9   Flatten the ends of the U-shaped wires with the flat side of the chasing hammer. Use
    the 1.25 mm hole-punch (or center punch, drill and #56 drill bit) to make 1 hole in each
    flattened end for the rivets. Use the holes in the U-shaped wires as a guide to punch or
    drill corresponding holes in each end of the larger copper strip. Insert 1 escutcheon pin
    through each hole in the U-shaped wires and strip. Snip the pins on the other side of the
    strip, leaving just enough to form a rivet. Rivet the pins in place. [figure 7].

10 Bend to the larger copper strip to form a C-shape [figure 8].

11 Attach one end of the bracelet to the short loop, then pinch the loop closed with flat-
    nose pliers [figure 9].

12 Patina the bracelet with liver of sulfur, if desired, then polish and wear!

Gambler's Luck Necklace

DESIGNED BY:
Kim St. Jean

FINISHED SIZE:
13¼" long x 3¼" wide
(33.65 cm x 8.25 cm)

AS A KID I HAD A DYED RABBIT'S FOOT FOR LUCK.
I got to thinking about good luck, rabbits, and what you need
good luck for. I had several beads that had a gambling theme,
so I pulled them out. I added the rabbit head, and then I thought
about what I would most want if I won a jackpot. I decided I
would want more time. So out came the watch faces.

materials

42mm vintage watch face

40x18mm bone rabbit-head bead

2 miniature dice beads

25x17mm bone playing-card bead

1 pair of copper etched wings (see spotlight)

6" (15.2 cm) of copper 18-gauge wire

2 brass ¹⁄₁₆" (1.5 mm) diameter 7 mm long
   micro screws

4 stainless steel 4 mm diameter nuts to match
   micro screws

4 copper ¹⁄₁₆" (1.5mm) tubular rivets (eyelets)

1 copper 5mm eyelet

1 brass 6mm washer

2 brass 7mm 16 gauge jump rings

1" of gunmetal 2mm rolo chain

20" (50.8 cm) of vintage brass chain

1 copper 8.5mm toggle clasp

tools

Etching tools & materials (see spotlight)

Jeweler's saw frame

#3/0 saw blades

Coarse sanding sponge

Liver of sulfur

#0000 steel wool

Spring loaded center punch

Flex shaft or drill

Drill bits: ¹⁄₁₆" (1.5 mm) and ¹⁄₈" (3.1 mm)

Small ball-peen hammer

Anvil or steel bench block

Safety mask

Scribe

Needle files

Butane micro torch

Bowl of water

Tweezers

Round-nose pliers

Chain-nose pliers

Flush cutters

1.25 mm hole-punch pliers

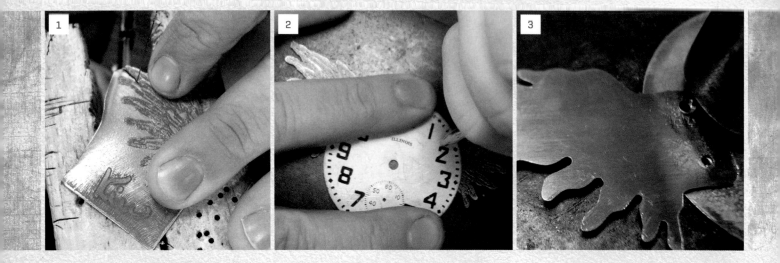

1. Saw out the shape of the etched wings (see spotlight) using a jeweler's saw frame and #3/0 saw blade, making sure to leave enough of a copper surface on each wing to attach it to the back of the watch face [figure 1].

2. Sand the edges of the wings smooth with the coarse sanding sponge. Patina the wings in a warm liver of sulfur solution, rinse with water, then dry. Use the #0000 steel wool to remove the excess oxidation and achieve the desired patina.

3. Align the watch face on top of the wing cutouts. Center punch and drill 4 holes (2 per wing) through the watch face and wings with a $1/16$" (1.5 mm) drill bit. Having 2 rivets per wing prevents them from spinning around [figure 2].

4. Thread one $1/16$" (1.5mm) tubular rivet through the front of the watch face and the top hole drilled in the wing. Flip the pendant over and use a center punch to flare the end of the tube rivet. Gently tap down the edges with a small ball-peen hammer. Repeat for the other top rivet hole and the 2 bottom rivet holes [figure 3].

5. Drill a hole in the center of the playing-card bead with the $1/16$" (1.5 mm) drill bit. Position the rabbit-head and playing-card embellishments in place on the watch face. Use a scribe to mark through the holes onto the watch face for the rivet locations. Mark the spot at the bottom of the watch face where you will dangle the dice. Center punch all 3 hole locations on the watch face. Drill the holes for the playing card and rabbit head with a $1/16$" (1.5 mm) drill bit. Drill the bottom hole for the chain with $1/8$" (3.1 mm) drill bit. File away any burrs with a fine-tip round file [figure 4].

TIP

Bone is very easy to drill; however, be sure to wear a mask—it smells terrible and is not good for you.

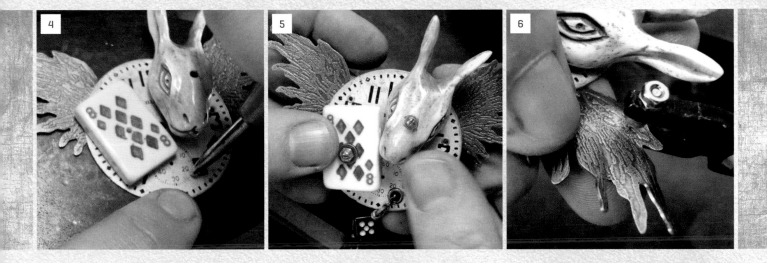

6 Place the copper eyelet through the front of the bottom hole. Turn the watch face over and use a center punch to flare the edges of the eyelet. Use a small ball-peen hammer to flatten the edges.

7 Use a butane micro torch to ball up the ends of two 3" [7.6 cm] pieces of 10-gauge copper wire. Quench the pins in a bowl of water; dry. Or, you may use 2 premade copper 3" [7.6 cm] head pins.

8 Thread the 1" [2.5 cm] piece of gunmetal rolo chain through the bottom eyelet. Place 1 die on each head pin and attach them to each end of the chain with a wrapped loop.

9 Thread 1 nut onto 1 micro screw. Thread the screw through the head of the rabbit and then through the watch face. Flip the pendant over and thread another nut on the end of the screw. Tighten the nut with chain-nose pliers. Trim the screw, leaving 1mm of thread above the nut. File the end flat. Use the small ball-peen hammer to flare the end of the screw out and over the nut.

10 Thread 1 nut and 1 decorative washer onto the remaining micro screw. Thread the screw through the front of the playing card and then through the watch face. Thread on another nut and tighten it. Finish the back as you did in Step 9 [figure 5].

11 Use the round-nose pliers to shape the wings. Punch a hole in each wing with the 1.25 mm hole-punch pliers to attach the chain [figure 6].

12 Open 2 jump rings and insert one into each wing hole. Cut the vintage chain in half and attach each half to each jump ring. Attach the toggle clasp to each end of the vintage chain.

TIP

I have drilled an indentation in the corner of my anvil the size of a screw head. I place the screw head in the indentation when I'm hammering to prevent it from flattening.

Etching on Copper, Brass, and Nickel Silver

Safety first! Wear safety glasses, nitrile gloves, and an apron while working with ferric chloride. Wear a mask when sanding away the excess etching solution. Have proper ventilation and *do not inhale the vapors.*

materials

Copper 24-gauge sheet (or brass or nickel silver sheet)

Rubber stamp of wings

StāzOn black ink

tools

Safety glasses

Nitrile gloves

Apron

Newspaper

Dishwashing soap

Green kitchen scrub pad

Paper towels

Glass or plastic dish (use this dish only for etching)

Ferric chloride

Packing tape

Kitchen timer

Toothpick

Bowl of water

Baking soda

Safety mask

Sanding sponge

ALSO USED IN:

Garden Wind Gong Pendant, page 034

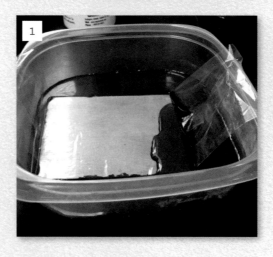

1 Cover your work surface with newspaper.

2 Clean your metal thoroughly with dishwashing soap and a green kitchen scrub pad. You want to remove all oils and dirt from the surface of the metal. When you rinse away the soap, you should see the water sheet off of the metal surface, not bead up. Take care not to touch the surface of the metal after cleaning it. Use paper towels to dry the metal.

3 Apply your resist material (StāzOn Ink, red paint pen, permanent marker, stickers, etc.) to the surface of the metal and let it dry completely.

4 Pour about a ½" (1.3 cm) of ferric chloride into a shallow glass or plastic container.

5 Cover the entire back of the metal with packing tape.

6 Pull off another piece of packing tape that is 4" (10.1 cm) longer than your container is wide. Place the taped back of the metal in the middle of the sticky side of the long piece of packing tape. You want to create a "trapeze" of tape so that the metal is submerged in the surface tension of the ferric chloride, but not completely covered. Slide the metal piece face down into the ferric chloride and suspend it across the top of the container, attaching the tape to the sides [figure 1].

7 Set a timer for 1 hour.

8 Check the etching action by lifting the taped metal up and sliding a toothpick down the design to feel for thickness of etch.

9 If you are satisfied with the depth of the etching, remove the metal from the etching solution and place it in a bowl of water with 2 teaspoons of baking soda in it.

10 Remove the metal from the baking soda bowl and scrub it thoroughly with a green scrub pad and soap and water.

11 Put on the mask. Use the sanding sponge to sand the design and remove the remainder of the etching solution.

12 Neutralize the remaining etching solution with a baking soda and water solution: 2 cups of water and ¼ cup baking soda. Dispose at the nearest hazardous-waste disposal site.

Riveted Flower Rings

DESIGNED BY: **Tracy Stanley**

FINISHED SIZE:
**7/8" diameter x 7/8" high
(2.2 cm di x 2.2 cm)**

IT'S ALL ABOUT THE FUN! These flower rings are as much fun to make as they are to wear—just a little bit of spring on your fingers.

materials

3" x 3" (7.6 x 7.6 cm) of 24-gauge brass, copper, and silver sheet

1/16" (1.5mm) short and long copper, brass, or silver mini eyelets

3" (7.6 cm) of 1/16" (1.5 mm) tubing

Spacers with holes large enough to fit 1/16" (1.5 mm) tubing

tools

Graphing ruler

Metal shears

Plastic mallet

Steel bench block and pad

Texturing hammers

Design stamps

Household-type hammer

Brass texturing plates (optional)

Masking tape

Half-round flat file, #2 cut

Needle files

Liver of sulfur

Pro-Polish polishing pad

Large (13, 16, and 20 mm) stepped wrap-and-tap forming pliers

Ultrafine-tip permanent marker

1.8 mm hole-punch pliers

Metal ring mandrel or mini anvil

Chasing hammer, Fretz large embossing hammer, or riveting hammer

Circle template

Dapping block and punches

Jeweler's saw frame

#0/3 saw blades

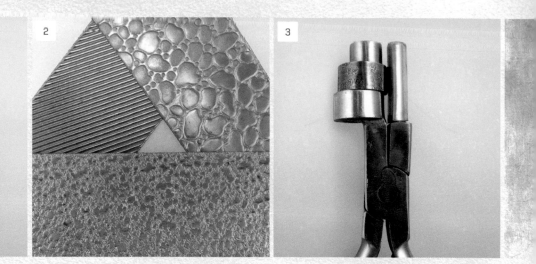

TIP

You can also use brass texture plates, commonly used for PMC patterning. These plates are available in assorted patterns and give the look of metal that has been rolled through a rolling mill. Place the brass texture plate on a bench block under your blank sheet metal, texture side up, and hold it in place with masking tape. Use a heavy household-type hammer to hammer firmly all over your metal piece. Check to see if you are getting the desired texture by lifting the metal piece up. If you need more texture, continue hammering [figure 2].

1 Measure and cut a strip of metal that is 3" (7.6 cm) in length and $3/8$–$1/2$" (9.5 mm–1.2 cm) in width for the ring band. Flatten the strip with the plastic mallet. Place the band on the bench block and tap gently with texturing hammers to create the desired effect. You can also use multiple design stamps to create texture or use brass texture plates [figure 1].

2 File the corners of the strip, patina with liver of sulfur, and clean with a Pro-Polish polishing pad. It is easier to patina with liver of sulfur and clean up the piece before forming. Use the largest step (20 mm) on the wrap-and-tap pliers to roll the strip halfway over. Flip the strip around and wrap to complete the circle. There must be at least a $1/4$" (6.3 mm) overlap [figure 3].

3 Slip the band on your finger and squeeze to determine your size. Draw a line on the band with the permanent marker where it overlaps. Slip the band off your finger. Hold the band in position and use the 1.8 mm metal hole-punch pliers to punch a hole through the 2 band layers, close to one of the front edge corners.

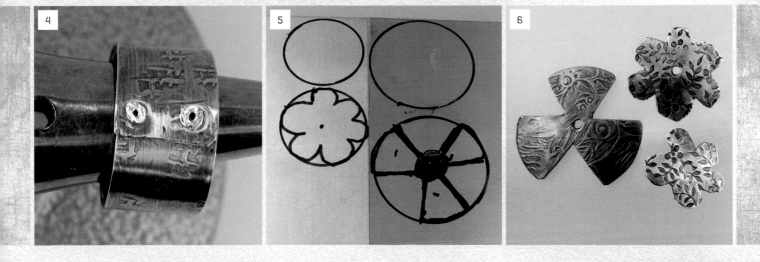

4   Place a 1/16" (1.5mm) eyelet into that hole and then place the whole piece on a ring mandrel. If you don't have a ring mandrel, this can be done on a mini anvil. Tap gently on the eyelet with the ball end of your chasing hammer, Fretz large embossing hammer, or riveting hammer until the end spreads out flat. Punch a second hole on the opposite corner of the band and put a second eyelet in and tap down [figure 4].

5   Draw a 1" (2.5 cm) circle on your choice of sheet metal with the permanent marker. Draw the petal design within the circle. The petal design is up to you. Draw 2 more petal shapes using ¾" (1.9 cm) circles and ½" (1.2 cm) circles for the outer circle dimensions on any other piece of sheet metal you desire. I used different types of metal for added interest [figure 5].

6   Cut the petals out with metal shears. Use a plastic mallet to flatten the petals. Place each petal on the bench block and tap gently with texturing hammers or design stamps to create texture. File the edges to smooth and shape. Patina the petals with liver of sulfur. Punch holes in the center of each petal with the 1.8 mm metal hole-punch [figure 6].

7   Place each of the petals (texture side up) in a dapping block hole, place the matching punch on top and tap with the hammer to dome the petals into a cup shape **[figure 7]**.

8   Punch a hole in the ring band with the 1.8 mm hole-punch where you want to attach your flower petals. You can punch on the front of the band to cover your rivets or on the opposite side **[figure 8]**.

9   Take a 3" (7.6 cm) piece of $1/16$" (1.5 mm) tubing. Holding it upright, gently tap the end with the ball end of a chasing hammer or a Fretz large embossing hammer. This will spread out the end just enough to hold it in place on the ring band.

10 Place the tubing through the ring band and stack the largest petal on the tubing, then a spacer bead and another petal, and a spacer bead and another petal. Add a decorative spacer on top for the final piece. Use the permanent marker to draw a line about $1/32$" (.79 mm) above the last top spacer **[figure 9]**.

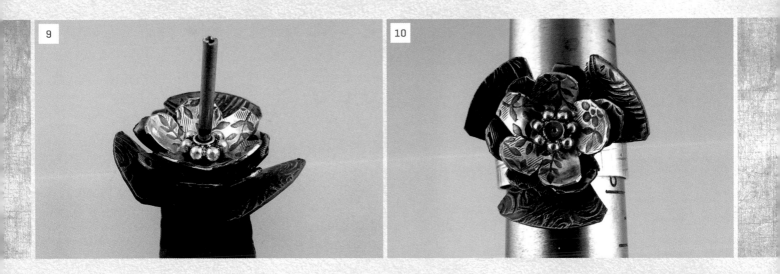

note

It is very important that the final spacer fit snug to the tubing.

11 Remove the pieces from the tubing and cut the tubing on the mark using the jeweler's saw frame and a #0/3 saw blade. Insert the tubing in the hole of the ring band from the inside and slip the band on a ring mandrel. Place the pieces and spacers back on the tube and very gently tap on the end of the tubing to flare it out and hold everything in place [figure 10].

Option: For the simple version, use a long 1/16" (1.5mm) eyelet instead of tubing. Insert the eyelet into the ring band and place however many petals will fit on to the eyelet. You may or may not be able to add the spacers in between. Tap on the end of the eyelet to hold the pieces on.

Reversible Mini Book Locket

DESIGNED BY:
Beth Taylor

FINISHED SIZE:
14¾" long x 1⅛" wide
[37.47 cm x 2.86 cm]

I SET OUT TO CREATE A LOCKET that lovers of bolder, less traditional jewelry, including myself, would love to wear. The result is this book-inspired locket, each page designed to hold a favorite photo that can be easily inserted and removed. Not too sweet, yet still full of heart, this locket is definitely worthy of your favorite mementos!

materials

Sterling silver sheet: 22- and 24-gauge

Brass sheet: 20- and 24-gauge

Tin from tin cans

2 oxidized sterling silver 8" [20.3 cm] pieces of 18-gauge wire

14-gauge sterling silver round beaded or twisted wire

1½" [3.8 cm] of sterling silver ⅛" [3.1 mm] bezel wire

8" [20.3 cm] of .024" flexible beading wire such as Soft Flex

8 #00-90 miniature brass fillister-head bolts

5 #0-80 miniature brass fillister-head bolts

4 miniature brass nails, .020" diameter

2 sterling silver 2x2mm crimp tubes

3 sterling silver 3mm ID 18-gauge jump rings

1 oxidized sterling silver 3" [7.6 cm] 22-gauge head pin

Small bead of your choice

Chain of your choice

tools

Fine-tip permanent marker

1 sheet of label paper

Scissors

Jeweler's saw frame

Saw blades: #2/0 and #4/0

Bench pin

Joyce Chen kitchen scissors

Rawhide mallet

Flex shaft or Dremel tool

Drill bits: #52, #55 #57, and #75

Wood block for drilling

Ring clamp

Adhesive remover such as Goo Gone [optional]

High-speed cylinder burr [6+ mm]

Half-round/flat file

Square and triangle needle files

Ruler

Center punch [slim automatic or regular]

400- and 600-grit wet/dry sandpaper for metal

Steel ⅛" [3.1 mm] letter and number stamp set

Household hammer

Steel bench block or anvil

Miniature flathead screwdriver

Flush cutters

Riveting hammer

Liver of sulfur

Soft scrub brush

Dishwashing liquid

Pro-Polish polishing pad

Miniature chamois or muslin buff [optional]

ZAM polish [optional]

Windex

Clear Krylon acrylic non-yellowing spray-on sealer

Round bezel mandrel

2 pairs of chain-nose pliers

Round-nose pliers

Crimping pliers

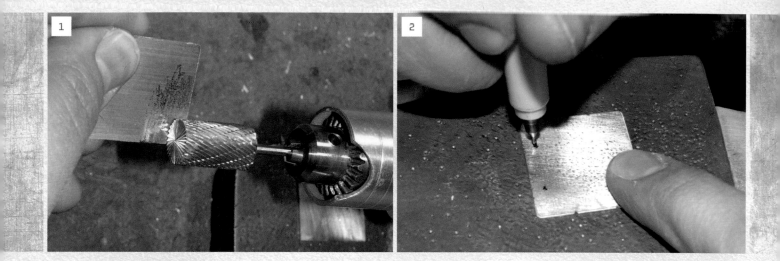

Locket Cover (front & back)

Locket Page

Photo Frame

Heart for Back Cover

1 You will be making a front and back cover along with 2 interior pages that hold your photos using the templates at left. Copy 2 "locket cover" templates onto label paper, cut them out, and affix them to the 22-gauge sterling silver sheet. Using a jeweler's saw frame and #2/0 saw blade, saw out the 2 templates.

2 Copy the template for the locket page onto label paper, cut it out, and affix it to the 24-gauge brass sheet. Using the jeweler's saw frame and #4/0 saw blade or Joyce Chen scissors, cut out the template. Flatten the cut metal with a rawhide mallet if necessary.

3 Copy the template for 2 photo frames onto label paper, cut them out, and affix them to the 24-gauge sterling silver sheet. Cut out along the outside of the template using the jeweler's saw frame and #4/0 saw blade or Joyce Chen scissors. Flatten with a rawhide mallet if necessary. Use a #55 drill bit to drill a pilot hole on the inside of the frame. Use a jeweler's saw frame and #4/0 saw blade to cut out the interior shape.

4 Use a permanent marker to mark the width of 1 locket cover on a strip of brass 20-gauge sheet. This will be the length of your brass strip. The width of the strip should be 6mm. Saw out the strip with a jeweler's saw frame and #2/0 blade.

5 Remove the label paper from all of the pieces. Use an adhesive remover such as Goo Gone if necessary.

6 Add texture to both sides of all of the metal pieces, using a flex shaft and cylinder burr [figure 1].

7 File all the pieces, including the inside of the frames. Use a square needle file inside the corners of the frames if necessary. Make random notches to distress the edges of the front and back cover and inside pages with a triangle needle file.

8 Mark and drill holes in the front cover for wire hinges: Measure in 8 mm from the left side and down 1.5 mm from the top. Mark with the permanent marker and center punch. Repeat on the right side. Drill the holes where marked, using a #52 drill bit [figure 2].

9. Place the front cover on top of the back cover. Using the front cover as a template, transfer the location of the holes onto the back cover with the marker. Center punch and drill the holes with a #52 drill bit. Center punch and drill a hole on the back cover, centered and about 2mm from the bottom edge for the bead dangle. Drill with a #55 drill bit.

10. Lay the back cover on your work surface with the inside of the cover facing up. Place one of the brass pages on top of the cover, aligned with the top edge of the back cover, and centered horizontally. Hold the pages firmly in place and transfer the location of the holes with a marker onto the brass page using the cover page as your template. Center punch and drill the holes with a #52 drill bit. Repeat for second inside page.

11. Sand all the pieces using 400-grit then 600-grit wet/dry sandpaper.

12. Prepare and stamp the brass strip for the front cover: Measure in 3 mm from the left edge of the strip and mark the vertical center with the marker. Center punch on the mark and repeat on the right end of the strip.

13. Measure 2.5 mm from the indent on the left and mark with the marker. Place your first letter stamp to the immediate right of this mark, centered vertically. I imprinted "My Heart." Strike the stamp with the flat side of the household hammer. The letter should be crisply imprinted on the brass strip. Repeat with all the remaining letters. Flatten the strip with the rawhide mallet if necessary. File the edges straight after stamping if necessary. Drill the indents with a #52 drill bit [figure 3].

14. Attach the "My Heart" strip to the front cover: Place the brass strip squarely in the center of the front cover. Mark the placement of the right hole using the strip as a template. Center punch and drill with a #55 drill bit. Widen the hole slightly with a square or triangle needle file. Insert a #0-80 fillister-head bolt through both the strip and the cover, using a miniature screw driver. Place the piece face down on the bench block and snip off the excess shaft of the bolt, leaving only a tiny amount of excess material. Rivet using the riveting hammer. Repeat with the second hole [figure 4].

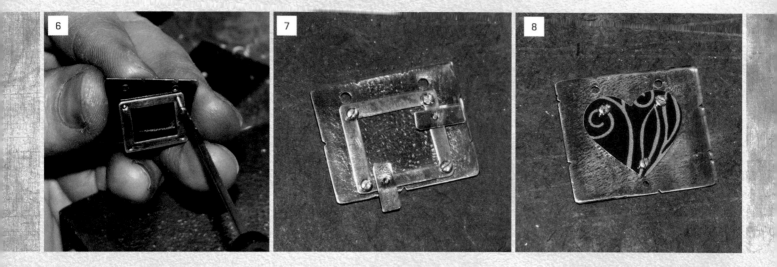

15 Rivet the frames to the inside pages: Center punch a mark in each corner of both frames. Drill each mark with a #55 drill bit. Place 1 frame on the brass page just below the hinge holes, making sure the frame is centered [figure 5, previous page]. Mark the location of the top right hole using the marker and center punch. Drill the hole with a #57 drill bit. Slightly widen the hole by inserting and turning a triangle or square needle file. Insert a #00-90 brass bolt through the holes in the frame and cover using a miniature screwdriver. Snip off the excess shaft and rivet. Repeat with the lower left corner, then with the remaining two corners. Repeat with second page [figure 6].

16 Make the tabs for the interior pages: Texture the sterling silver ⅛" (3.1 mm) bezel wire using the flex shaft and cylinder burr. Cut four 6 mm pieces of bezel wire with Joyce Chen scissors. File the edges and sand with 400-grit then 600-grit wet/dry sandpaper.

17 Measure 3 mm from the end of all 4 tabs, center punch and drill with a #75 drill bit.

18 Take one of the pages. On the frame, measure 3 mm down from the bottom edge of the top right screw and mark with the center punch. Measure in 3 mm from the inside edge of the lower left screw; mark with the center punch. Drill both holes with a #75 drill bit. Repeat on the second page.

19 Place the tab with the shorter end facing toward the inside of the frame. Insert a miniature nail through the tab, frame, and page. Snip and rivet. Repeat with second tab and then repeat on second page [figure 7].

20 Oxidize both covers and both inside pages with liver of sulfur. Wash with a soft scrub brush and a drop of dishwashing liquid. Rinse and dry. Polish all the pages with a Pro-Polish pad to remove the excess patina. For a higher shine, polish using the flex shaft, miniature buff, and a bit of polish.

21 Copy the heart template onto label paper, cut it out, and affix it to the tin. Using Joyce Chen scissors, cut out the heart template from the tin. Remove the label paper, then file and sand the edges with 400-grit wet/dry sandpaper.

22 Mark, center punch, and drill 3 holes in the heart for the rivets with a #52 drill bit. Clean the tin heart with Windex. Seal with clear spray-on sealer; let dry.

TIP

Attach the label paper to the side of the tin without the design so the color doesn't come off.

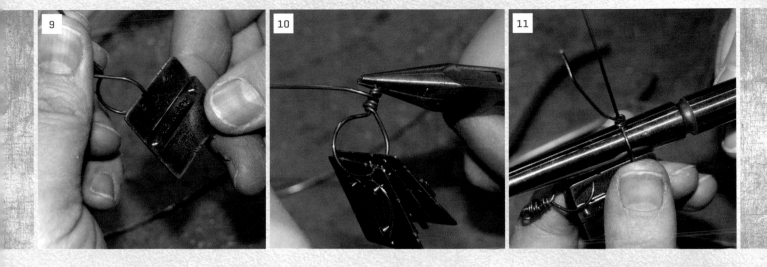

23 Center the heart on the outside of the back cover. Mark the placement of the top right hole with the marker and center punch. Drill the hole with a #55 drill bit. Widen the hole slightly with a triangle or square needle file.

24 Insert a #0-80 brass bolt through both the heart and the back cover. Snip off the excess shaft and rivet. Repeat with the bottom hole and then with the remaining upper left hole [figure 8].

25 Wrap one 8" (20.3 cm) piece of 18-gauge wire around the large part of the round bezel mandrel, leaving one end about 2½" (6.3 cm) long. Remove from the mandrel. Grasp the loop with the short end of the wire facing away from you. Make a 90-degree bend in the longer wire using chain-nose pliers. Slide the cover, then the inside page, and then the back cover onto the wire so they hang from the large loop [figure 9].

26 Use chain-nose pliers to grasp the loop at the top, holding both wires firmly in the jaws of the pliers. Wrap the shorter end of the wire around the longer wire three times, forming a large wrapped loop; snip off the excess wire.

27 Grasp the wire with the tip of the chain-nose pliers and bend the wire away from you at a 90-degree angle. Grasp the wire close to the pliers with round-nose pliers. Roll the pliers toward you so the wire is pointing straight at you. Grasp the wire with chain-nose pliers and wrap it around the round-nose pliers. Remove the round-nose pliers and grasp the wires at the bottom of the loop with the chain-nose pliers. Wrap the wire around itself and trim off the excess [figure 10].

28 Repeat Steps 25–27 with the second piece of 18-gauge wire. However, this time, when threading the pages onto the wire, line up all the pages first and insert the wire through all of the pages at the same time. If at any time your large loop becomes misshapen, simply slide it gently onto the bezel mandrel to reshape it. The loop "hinges" should be the same height, with the opening of both small loops facing sideways. Polish the loops with a Pro-Polish pad to remove the excess patina [figure 11].

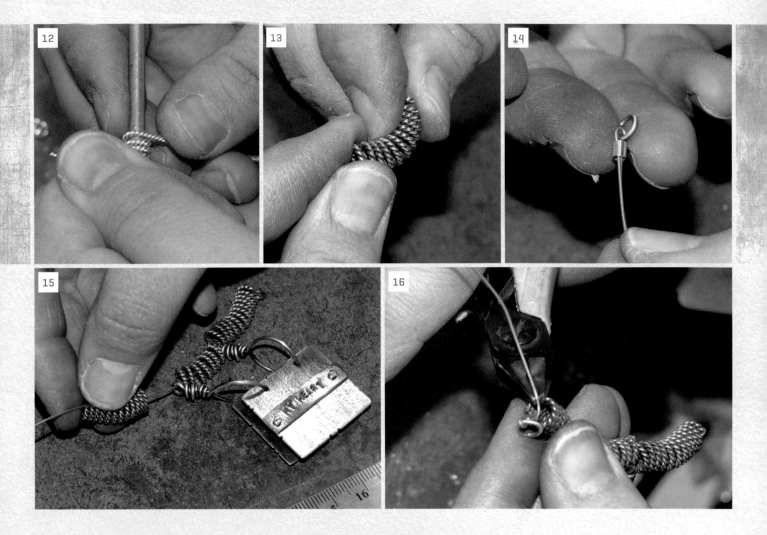

29 Wrap the 14-gauge beaded or twisted wire around the 4 mm round mandrel forming 3
coils: 2 should be about 18 mm long and 1 should be about 12 mm long [figure 12].

30 Darken the coils with liver of sulfur and clean with a Pro-Polish pad. Form each piece of
wrapped wire with your fingers into a slight "U" shape [figure 13].

31 Thread one 2x2mm crimp tube and 1 small jump ring onto the end of the 8" piece of
flexible beading wire. Pass the wire back through the crimp tube, then push the crimp
tube as close to the jump ring as possible. Secure the crimp with crimping pliers. Snip off
excess beading wire, leaving a small tail [figure 14].

32 Thread on 1 long coil, the right loop of the locket, the short piece of coiled wire, the left
loop of the locket, and finally the remaining long piece of coiled wire [figure 15].

33 Thread on another 2x2mm crimp tube and small jump ring. Pass the wire back through
the crimp tube and secure the crimp with crimping pliers. Snip off the excess beading
wire, leaving a small tail. Tuck the tail into the coiled wire section [figure 16].

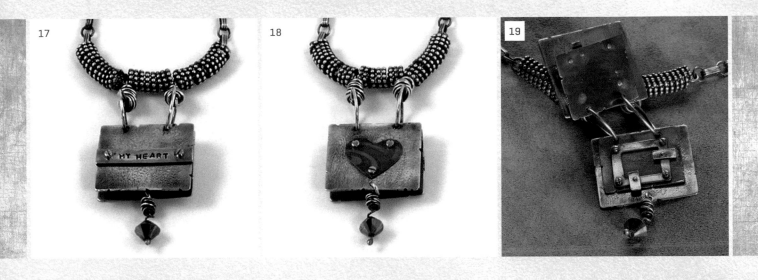

17   18   19

34 Open 1 jump ring on the end of the beading wire and add the chain of your choice; close the jump ring. Repeat with other side.

35 Create a bead dangle: Place the bead on a head pin and wrap the head pin several times around the round-nose pliers. Bend the wire so the spiral is perpendicular. Gently pull wire straight up to expand the spiral. Form a wrapped loop at the top of the wire and trim the excess. Open the remaining small jump ring, add the wrapped bead, and insert the jump ring into the hole on the bottom of the back cover; close the jump ring. Clean the wire with the Pro-Polish pad [figures 17, 18, and 19].

Photo Tips for Lockets

1   To size your photo, cut or shrink your photo to $^{13}/_{32}$" wide by $^3/_8$" high [1 cm x 0.95 cm].

2   Use photo-processing software to manipulate a digital image, making it just the right size for your locket. Or use a photocopier at an office-services store to reduce the image, then cut the photocopy to fit.

3   To protect your photo, use clear packing tape to laminate your image on both sides. You can also use self-stick laminating sheets, which will not yellow over time.

4   Slide your photo into the frame, behind the tabs. If the photo does not fit, remove and trim accordingly. Once you have a good fit, press around the edge of the photo using the end of a paper clip to ensure the photo is placed securely.

Contributing Artists

Dawn Bergmaier
dawnbergmaier.com

Dawn Bergmaier creates a line of handmade sterling silver jewelry, combining the individuality of the craft artist with the clean design approach of the fine jeweler. She searches for inspiration through industrial design and strives to find a sense of order and clarity in form and shape. Dawn received her BFA from Temple University's Tyler School of Art and currently works in her home studio in the Philadelphia area. She also teaches at Moore College of Art and Design in Philadelphia and at the Main Line Art Center in Haverford, Pennsylvania.

Janice Berkebile
wiredarts.net

Being a native to the Pacific Northwest, Janice is inspired by the organic forms found in nature, Japanese motifs, textile techniques, and the sinuous lines found in the Art Nouveau movement. Her focus is wire and metalwork. Janice's passion is becoming intimate with the subtleties of this medium and sharing these techniques with her students.

Lisa and Scott Cylinder
lisaandscottcylinder.com

Lisa and Scott Cylinder began collaborating in 1988. They have created limited production studio multiples under the auspices of "Chickenscratch" for the past twenty-one years. They take a no-holds-barred attitude about materials and techniques and create a very limited number of highly collected art-jewelry pieces. Their works display a dichotomy of the man-made and the natural worlds. Lisa and Scott are always looking for that elusive inspiration from which their next concept will emerge.

Robert Dancik
fauxbone.com

Robert Dancik holds a Masters degree in sculpture from Northern Illinois University, and a BA in fine art from Adelphi University. He has been an artist/teacher for more than thirty years and is presently an adjunct professor of education at Pace University. Robert has taught people from kindergarten to graduate school while exhibiting his jewelry and sculpture in museums and galleries across the United States and in Europe, Japan, and Australia. He teaches workshops at art centers in the United States and abroad. Robert lives in Lostwithiel, Cornwall, United Kingdom where he teaches, is an avid cook, and collector of toys, maps, and compasses.

Karen Dougherty
karendougherty.com

Karen is a graduate of the University of South Carolina Art Studio program. She began her career as a print graphic designer. For the last thirteen years she has worked full time as a designer for Interweave for their gem and jewelry group of magazines and events. She has made lampworked glass beads and jewelry as a hobby for the last fifteen years. Making jewelry and sharing her passion for it is now her full-time occupation.

Connie Fox
jatayu.com

Connie Fox has been making metal jewelry for the last thirteen years, and she has been teaching since 2001. Her classes focus on large-scale wirework, cold connections, metal fabrication, jewelry design, and enameling. She has served as an adjunct professor with San Diego Community College Continuing Education and teaches Beginning Fabrication Skills.

Thomas Mann
thomasmann.com

A professional artist for over forty years, Thomas Mann is best known for his "Techno-Romantic"™ style of jewelry, which juxtaposes contemporary technology and construction techniques with historical romantic imagery. Originally from Pennsylvania, the artist exhibited his work at Jazz Fest in 1977 and has called New Orleans home ever since. He continues to show his work at nationally juried craft and art events and in gallery and museum exhibitions. Thomas currently teaches a series of hands-on jewelry-making workshops as well as his now twenty-year old workshop Design for Survival™-Entrepreneurial Thinking and Tactics, for artists in all mediums.

Lisa Niven-Kelly
beaducation.com

Lisa Niven Kelly is an award-winning artist who finds joy in all things beads. Currently, her work focuses on wirework, into which she incorporates beads whenever possible.

She has been teaching beadwork and wirework for more than fifteen years. These days, you will find her mainly sticking close to home with her two young daughters, managing her business, Beaducation.com. Lisa is the author of *Stamped Metal Jewelry* (Interweave).

Kate Richbourg

Kate has fostered creativity in the bead industry for nearly fifteen years through the teaching and development of classes at various stores and bead conferences throughout the country. Her jewelry designs have appeared in several books and magazines. Most recently, Kate has made several appearances on the cable show *DIY Jewelrymaking*. Former owner of Beadissimo in San Francisco, Kate is now director of education for beaducation.com.

Marthe Roberts-Shea

Marthe has had a lifelong interest in jewelry making. Her grandfather, a Russian immigrant, became a jeweler at Tiffany & Co. in New York City. He died before she was born, but the jewelry that he left behind both intrigued and inspired her desire to explore jewelry making as an art form.

Already an accomplished artist and graduate of Moore College of Art, Marthe's sculptural woodworking and functional furniture has been shown in galleries nationally and in the Philadelphia Museum of Art. Her work is currently in several private collections in Washington, D.C., New York, New Mexico, and Pennsylvania. The jewelry she makes combines her design skills and ability to visualize unique mixes of textures, shapes, and finishes into one-of-a-kind pieces.

Richard Salley
rsalley.com

Richard has a lifelong interest in art and making things. He worked as an assistant to metal sculptor Malcom Moran where he learned about metalwork. He taught elementary, middle, and high school during his thirty-two years as an educator, and he incorporated art into as many lessons as he could along the way. Richard's interests include digital art, mixed-media collage/assemblage, sculpture, and jewelry. Richard prefers to work with alternative materials and non-traditional techniques when creating art.

Julie Sanford
juliesanforddesigns.com

Julie Sanford's fascination with the arts began at a young age, as she assisted in her mother's ceramics business and watched from afar as her father collected stones and fashioned them into small works of art. She grew up in Kalamazoo and spent her school years exasperating teachers with her tendency to wander off into an inner world of magic and imagination. As an adult, Julie attended art school and, ironically, became a teacher herself. She spent many years honing her craft. Julie teaches silversmithing in her Grand Haven studio and resides in western Michigan with her husband and three sons. Her work is displayed nationally in museum shops, jewelry stores, and galleries.

Kim St. Jean
kimstjean.com,
expressive-impressions.com

After teaching in the public school system for ten years, Kim decided to explore jewelry making, and it was not long after that, she combined her creativity with her love of teaching and began teaching others how to make jewelry. Kim has taught for five years at Swarovski's Crystallized® event in Tucson. This year, she was named one of Swarovski's Ambassadors. Kim owns Expressive Impressions Inc. with her husband, Norm, in Charlotte, North Carolina.

Tracy Stanley
wiredarts.net

Tracy has been teaching beading and wireworking techniques for over seventeen years. She loves organic elements and brings them into her work. She rarely plans her pieces, rather she allows herself to follow a path and let things fall together naturally. Kim is a big believer in quality tools and solid techniques. She enjoys passing this on to her students so that they, too, can make quality pieces that are structurally sound, creating pieces that they can be proud of.

Beth Taylor
aquirkofart.com

A metalsmith and jewelry artist for more than eight years, Kim's background includes a mix of college-level metalsmithing and art courses, workshops, and self-taught methods. Kim is also a member of the Pennsylvania Guild of Craftsmen and the Pennsylvania Society of Goldsmiths.

Resources

A Grain of Sand

PO Box 3214
Mooresville, NC 28117
agrainofsand.com
(704) 660-3125

Vintage Chain

Project:
- Gambler's Luck Necklace, page 120

Beaducation Inc.

1347 Laurel St.
San Carlos, CA 94070
beaducation.com
(650) 654-7791

Design stamps, books, online classes, jewelry-making supplies

Projects:
- Medallion Bracelet, page 040
- Double-sided Pendant, page 106
- Riveted Flower Rings, page 126

Deb Jemmott

269 Solar View Dr.
San Marcos, CA 92069
debjemmott.com
(760) 744-8099

Brass riveting block (in the "tools" section, pages 20–21)

Project:
- Medallion Bracelet, page 040

Electronics Express

365 Blair Rd.
Avenel, NJ 07001
elexp.com
(800) 972-2225

Ferric chloride for etching

Project:
- Garden Wing Gong Pendant, page 034

Jatayu

1761 Hotel Cir. S., Ste. 208
San Diego, CA 92108-3318
jatayu.com
(888) 350-6481

Cold connection jewelry-making supplies and tools

Projects:
- Medallion Bracelet, page 040
- Cold Fusion Necklace, page 098

Jewelry Gems and Stones LLC

PO Box 428
Townville, SC 29689
jewelrygemsandstonesllc.com
(864) 972-1823

Dice beads

Project:
- Gambler's Luck Necklace, page 120

Kim St. Jean

10615 Industrial Dr., Ste. 100
Pineville, NC 28134
expressive-impressions.com
(704) 962-3496

Beads, kits, chain, findings, watch parts

Project:
- Gambler's Luck Necklace, page 120

Metalliferous

34 W. 46th St.
New York, NY 10036
metalliferous.com
(212) 944-0909

Textured sheet metal, metal shapes, screening

Project:
- Medallion Bracelet, page 040

Microfasteners

24 Cokesbury Rd., Ste. 2
Lebanon, NJ 08833
microfasteners.com
(800) 892-6917

Miniature nuts and bolts

Project:
- Medallion Bracelet, page 040

Micromark

340 Snyder Ave.
Berkeley Heights, NJ 07922
micromark.com
(800) 225-1066

Miniature brass nails

Project:
- Trio Bangles with Recycled Tin Charms, page 058

Objects and Elements

16128 Old Snohomish-Monroe Rd.
Snohomish, WA 98290
objectsandelements.com
(206) 965-0373

Assorted jewelry-making supplies

Project:
- Riveted Flower Ring, page 126

Reactive Metals

PO Box 890
Clarkdale, AZ 86324
reactivemetals.com
(800) 876-3434

Miniature brass bolts

Project:
- Trio Bangles with Recycled Tin Charms, page 058

Index

Bend and twist

your ideas into beautiful jewelry with these insightful and creative resources from Interweave

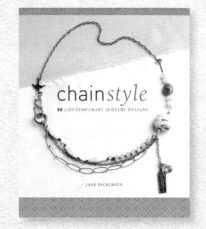

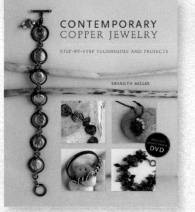

Chain Style
50 Contemporary Jewelry Designs
Jane Dickerson
ISBN 978-1-59668-150-7
$19.95

Contemporary Copper Jewelry with DVD
Step-by-Step Techniques and Projects
Sharilyn Miller
ISBN 978-1-59668-289-4
$26.95

Mixed Metals
Creating Contemporary Jewelry with Silver, Gold, Copper, Brass, and More
Danielle Fox and Melinda Barta
ISBN 978-1-59668-092-0
$22.95